The Zebra Book of Famous Men

This is a collection of short
biographies of men, famous
throughout history.
Scientists, explorers, statesmen
and artists; all can be found here.
Some are remembered for the
good they did, others for their
bad deeds, but all have made
their mark on history.

Cover illustration by Desmond Clover.

The Zebra Book of Famous Men

Plantagenet Somerset Fry

Illustrated by Desmond Clover

Evans Brothers Limited London

Published by Evans Brothers Limited
Montague House, Russell Square,
London, W.C.1.

Set in 11 on 12 point Baskerville
Printed in Great Britain
by Cox and Wyman Ltd.,
London, Reading and Fakenham

CSD SBN 237 35249 4   PRA 2943
PB SBN 237 44589 1

Introduction

This is a book about 125 of the most famous men in world history. You will notice that it does not include kings or emperors of the past 500 years or so (except for Napoleon who was more than just a ruler). This is because up to about 1700, or later in some lands, there were so many kings who played a very important part in their own countries and in the world, and to include them here would unbalance this book. They deserve a volume of their own.

Perhaps you will find some of your heroes – or villains – left out of this book. It is never possible to please everybody, though one should always strive to do so, and the names included are those judged to be preferred by the majority of children.

Plantagenet Somerset Fry

Adam, Robert (1728–1792), Scottish architect

Robert Adam was the most famous of four Scottish brothers who became architects. As a young man he visited Italy at a time when all Europe was talking about the amazing discoveries at Pompeii and Herculaneum. These were two famous towns not far from Naples which had been completely engulfed by the eruption of the volcano Vesuvius, in AD 79. When they were excavated many buildings were found in almost perfect condition, and from these Robert Adam, along with other European architects, was able to study Roman building techniques.

The result was what is called the Classical Revival in architecture, when architects began to design exteriors and interiors in the Roman style. Adam was the greatest of the British architects to adopt the style and among his buildings are Osterley Park, Middlesex; Harewood House, Yorkshire; and the Adelphi in London's Strand. He also designed furniture and his styles, which were often copied, are known as Adam furniture.

Alexander the Great (356–323 BC), Greek conqueror

Alexander was only twenty when he succeeded his father Philip as king of Macedonia, a small state in northern Greece, in 336 BC. Within ten years this tough, energetic man had made himself master of all the lands between Greece and India. It was the largest empire the world had known.

As a youth Alexander had proved himself a splendid commander in his father's army, not least because of his willingness to share the hardships of war with his troops. No sooner had he become king, when he marshalled an army and led it into Asia Minor. In a remarkable series of campaigns he conquered Syria, Phoenicia and Egypt (where he founded the city of Alexandria). At Arbela in Persia, then the mightiest kingdom in the Near East, he crushed its king, Darius III, seized his throne, put his own officers into the highest state positions, and married a Persian princess, Roxana. Then he set out for India, reaching the river Indus in 326.

Alexander planned to move on towards China, but a rebellion in Persia made him turn back to Babylon where he caught a dangerous fever and died.

Alfred the Great (849–899), king of England
Alfred was the only English king to be called the Great. Soldier, statesman, lawgiver, scholar, writer, inventor, he ruled so well that for generations afterwards his reign was recalled with pride and affection.

Alfred was born at Wantage, the youngest of the sons of king Aethelwulf (839–856). At twenty-one, he succeeded his brother Aethelred I and took over a kingdom ravaged and divided by an unending stream of Viking invasions. For some years he ruled quietly in the West Country, gathering his forces, training and equipping them, and making them ready to deal a decisive blow against the enemy. Then, in 878, he brought the Viking leader,

Guthrum, to battle in Wiltshire where he won a crushing victory.

Alfred's terms were far-reaching and generous. Guthrum and his men had to accept Christianity. They could live north of a line from London to Chester but they must live in peace. Alfred then re-organised the government of the kingdom, instituted schools, began a programme of shipbuilding for defence, and started the Anglo-Saxon Chronicle, a continuing history of England which was kept going right up to 1154.

In his leisure hours he invented the candle clock, and he also translated several works from Latin into English. This remarkable ruler also codified English law. Many of his descendants proved almost as able as he.

Amundsen, Roald (1872–1928), Norwegian explorer

Amundsen found a North-West passage to the Pacific, north of the mainland of Canada. Not content with this discovery, he sought to find the South Pole. He discovered it in 1911, reaching it about a month before a team led by Britain's Captain Scott who was also on the same search.

Norwegians have for centuries been sea-faring people, with a special interest in exploration, and Amundsen was no exception. As a young boy he had dreamed of finding the north-west passage. He also wanted to find the North Pole, but an American naval officer, Robert Peary, got there first, in 1909.

In 1928, Amundsen, still devoted to polar exploring, flew a seaplane to the North Pole to search for the Italian explorer, Nobile, who had tried to fly an airship across the Pole and had got into trouble. Amundsen's plane crashed and he was never heard of again.

Andersen, Hans Christian (1805–1875), Danish author

Hans Andersen's father, a poor shoemaker, died when the boy was only eleven. This meant he could no longer go to school, so he set out for Copenhagen and decided to become a singer. Unfortunately, he could not sing well and no one wanted to pay him. He was nearly reduced to starvation but by chance he was spotted by the king who arranged for him to finish his education.

Once grown up, Andersen turned to writing and he concentrated on children's stories. In these he made a great success and wrote some of the loveliest – and occasionally the saddest – of tales. 'The Ugly Duckling' and 'The Tin Soldier' show he never forgot his own humble beginnings, nor the hardships he endured.

Archimedes (*c.* 287–212 BC), Greek mathematician
Archimedes is famous for having jumped out of his bath and run through the streets of Syracuse in Sicily shouting 'Eureka!', the Greek word for 'I have found it'. He had in fact, proved his theory that when a solid is weighed in air and then in a fluid the apparent loss of weight is equal to the weight of fluid displaced. This was demonstrated by Archimedes to Hiero, king of Syracuse, to prove that the gold crown the king was wearing had in fact got some base metal in it, for when it was immersed in water it did not displace the correct amount of water which a truly solid gold crown of the same size would have done.

Archimedes devised many other things. One was a theory of levers; another was how to calculate the volume of a sphere, that is, a ball. He also invented the helical screw for lifting water from one level up to another, and he invented a magnifying glass which directed the sun's rays closely together upon an object and so set it on fire.

Attila, king of the Huns (*c.* 406–453)
Attila was chief of a large horde of Huns from Russia who ravaged Europe in the fifth century AD, looking for some of the wealth they had heard existed in the Roman Empire.

In 447 Attila reached the gates of Constantinople, then the richest city in the world. As his hordes settled down to attack, there was an earthquake, and it frightened them. Representatives of the Byzantine emperor Theodosius II then set out from the city to persuade Attila to leave them alone, offering three tons of gold as an inducement. Attila accepted and moved off.

In 452 Attila stormed through Italy and came to Rome, threatening to sack it. Again he was persuaded to stay his hand, this time by the Pope, Leo I, who offered no bribes at all.

The next year Attila died and was given a magnificent funeral.

Augustus (63 BC–AD 14), first Roman emperor
Caius Julius Caesar Octavianus was the great nephew of Julius Caesar (see page 20). Towards the end of his life the great dictator adopted Octavian as his son and heir and gave him a thorough grounding in statecraft. When Caesar was murdered, Octavian, along with Caesar's friend Mark Antony, took a terrible revenge and many leading Romans involved were executed. Then in 31 BC Octavian and Antony quarrelled and fought the battle of Actium, which Antony lost. Antony committed suicide, and Octavian was left master of the Roman world which stretched from northern Belgium to the borders of Persia.

The Roman people were tired of warfare and in 27 BC, through the Senate, they offered Octavian a new title, Princeps, that is, first person in the state. He also took the name 'Augustus', which means 'revered', and it remained the title of all succeeding emperors.

In forty years Augustus brought stability to the empire, strengthened its boundaries and provided an age of peace in which trade, industry, art and literature flourished. He also began a big programme of public building. Towards the end of his long life he said he had come to Rome when it was of brick and he was leaving it clad in marble.

Bach, Johann Sebastian (1685–1750), German composer
It is very difficult to say who was the greatest musical composer of

all time, but the majority of musicians would agree that there was no one quite like Johann Sebastian Bach. And you have only to listen to his music to understand why they feel this. Whether it is the forty-eight preludes and fugues, or the Brandenburg concertos, or the Mass in B Minor, every one of his works has a rhythm, a melody or a composite of melodies, and a technical excellence that is unequalled.

Bach was an organist and choir master for much of his life, and he was for a time organist to the Duke of Weimar. He played several instruments well, including the violin, the flute and the harpsichord, not to mention the organ.

Much of his work was of a religious nature. His appointments as organist demanded the composing of a cantata for nearly every festival of the church and in his time he produced almost three hundred of them. He also had to set the Good Friday story to music, and he did this to both the St. Matthew and the St. John version from the New Testament. His greatest piece of sacred music, however, which is also amongst the finest ever written anywhere, was the Mass in B Minor.

In his life he was never accorded the praise due to him and it was a century after his death before anyone recognised his genius.

Bacon, Friar Roger (*c.* 1214–1294), English monk and chemist
Although the Chinese had discovered how to make gunpowder nearly two thousand years ago, they did not learn to use it as an explosive force for blowing up buildings or discharging cannon balls or bullets. But in about 1250 an English monk, Roger Bacon, who was also an experimental chemist, carried out some tests with gunpowder. By compressing the mixture very tight and setting fire to it he found he could make it explode.

Here was a new force which could be employed to great effect in war, especially against castles and strongholds. But it was many years before gunpowder came into general use in fighting, and the first battle in which a cannon was fired was at Crecy, in 1346.

Bacon conducted experiments in many fields and invented a number of things. But his ingenuity earned him a lot of criticism and for years he was forbidden to practise his experiments.

Baden-Powell, Lord (1857–1941), founder of the Scout movement. Every Scout knows the Scouts' motto 'Be Prepared', but perhaps not so many now know that the first letters of the two words, B P, stand also for Baden-Powell, the founder of the Scout movement.

Major General Robert Baden-Powell had made his name famous as the heroic defender of Mafeking in the Second Boer War (1899–1902) in South Africa. He came back to England and was appointed Inspector-General of Cavalry, receiving a knighthood in 1908.

A year earlier Baden-Powell had organised a camping holiday for some boys, on which they spent much of their time learning and practising all manner of useful skills such as cooking on open fires, wood-cutting, knot-tying, tracking, even climbing rocks and building rope bridges. In 1908, he retired from the army with the rank of Lieutenant-General and wrote a book about the experiment and called it *Scouting for Boys*. It was an instant success and out of it was born the Scout movement which spread throughout the world, and of which he was, until his death in 1941, the Chief.

Becket, Thomas à (*c.* 1120–1170), Archbishop of Canterbury
When Henry II came to the English throne in 1154, his greatest friend was a London-born scholar and lawyer, Thomas à Becket. Soon after his coronation, the King appointed Becket Lord Chancellor, and for the next few years they worked well together reshaping the law and the government of the country. Then, in 1162, when the Archbishop of Canterbury died, Henry invited Becket to take his place. At first he was unwilling to accept as he foresaw that his duty as Archbishop would conflict with the King's will.

Almost at once Becket began to change completely in character. He became arrogant and morose. He also began to assert vigorously the rights and dignities of the Church and clergy.

At about this time the King was trying to reform the Church courts which were able to pass light sentences on people connected with the Church who committed crimes. The Pope refused to accept the reforms and Becket resisted so fiercely that Henry banished him. Six years later, he was asked to come back, but almost at once the two men quarrelled again. Unfortunately, Henry rashly sent four knights to Canterbury Cathedral to murder Becket, which they did on the altar steps, on 29th December, 1170. The shock of his murder spread through Europe soon after his death tales of miracles at his shrine were recorded, and he was made a saint in 1173.

Beethoven, Ludwig van (1770–1827), German composer
Imagine what it must be like to be a great musical composer – and to be so deaf that you cannot hear what you have written. This is what happened to Beethoven in the last seventeen years of his very productive life. When he was only twenty-eight he started to lose his hearing, and yet his last works are the greatest he composed.

Beethoven began to learn music when he was five and he was performing in public before he was ten. Mozart heard him and said he would become one of the world's great musicians – which he did.

In his twenties, Beethoven was thrilled by the new revolutionary spirit running through Europe following the French Revolution and he sought to apply this to his works. They became increasingly individual, conforming to no musical rules then in fashion. And as the individuality grew, so did its romance, its grandeur, its freedom from restraint. Soon he was out on his own, the dominating composer in Europe. It is doubly tragic to think of his last years of composing and playing such rich music and yet not being able to hear the applause which greeted it.

Bolivar, Simon (1783–1830), South American patriot

In the first years of the 19th century, following the French Revolution which pointed the way of freedom from oppression to many subject peoples, there was a general movement in South America to break away from the Spanish yoke. The principal leader in this movement was a Venezuelan-born patriot, Simon Bolivar, who in 1811 opened a campaign to drive out the Spanish. Bolivar had remarkable gifts as a leader and organiser of guerrilla warfare, and by 1819 he had driven the Spanish out of quite a part of South America and had set up a republic. Four years later he led another army of patriots against Spain, this time in Ecuador, and drove them out. In 1824 he did the same in Peru.

In 1826 the southern states of Peru combined to form an independent republic called Bolivia, after him. Bolivar wanted to unite all the new republics under him, but this was not popular. The various states had not thrown off Spanish dominion in order to take on another kind. All the same he was honoured everywhere as 'The Liberator' of the South American peoples.

Bonaparte, Napoleon (1769–1821), emperor of the French

Napoleon Bonaparte had an amazing career. Coming from a fairly humble home in Corsica, he rose to make himself emperor of the French (then the most powerful people in Europe) and master of a large part of Europe. He did all this before he was forty, but within six years of his fortieth birthday he was an exile, living thousands of miles away in an island off South Africa.

Napoleon entered the French army and by quickness of mind, his excellent head for detail, and boldness of decision, he reached the rank of colonel by the age of twenty-eight. He commanded French armies in northern Italy at the end of the 18th century and won great victories against superior numbers. Then he went to Egypt which he conquered, and thus became very dangerous to British interests in the Near East. His ambitions there were thwarted, however, by Lord Nelson (see page 68).

Napoleon returned to France to find the nation in chaos. The Revolution had died down and a Directory (or board of directors) ruled – and did not rule well. So, by skilful political manoeuvring and by playing on his great military fame, Napoleon managed to get himself made First Consul, then Sole Consul, and finally emperor of France (1804). In this capacity he strengthened central government, reorganised finance and set up a national bank. He founded the university of France, the order of the Legion of Honour, and removed, where he could, what was left of the hated privileges of feudalism. Henceforth men of talent rather than of birth should get to the top.

Then he began a programme of conquest in Europe. He won a series of victories in the field, at Austerlitz (1805), at Jena (1806) and at Friedland (1807), which rank with those of Marlborough (see page 62). He then put his brother on the Spanish throne, but Spanish patriots objected strongly and Napoleon's first reverse was in Spain, at Bailen, where one of his armies was crushed.

Five years later, led by Wellington (see page 87) allied forces drove him out of Spain. In 1812, meanwhile, he had invaded Russia and this had ended in disaster. Prussia and Austria thereupon rose against him and defeated him at Leipzig in 1813. In 1815 he made his last bid for victory at Waterloo, but was decisively beaten by Wellington. A few weeks later he was sent to exile in St. Helena, where he died in 1821.

Napoleon could have been a good influence on Europe. His first years as emperor were good for France. He recast the law and created the Napoleonic Code which in the main still exists. But his ambitions for conquest outweighed his desire to improve the nations which he threatened.

Boyle, the Hon. Robert (1627–1691), Irish chemist
Boyle is still known as the 'Father of Modern Chemistry', and one of the most important laws of gases is called Boyle's Law. This says that the volume of a given amount of gas at constant temperature varies inversely with the pressure, and it is a basic law of gas chemistry.

Boyle was the son of an Anglo-Irish peer, the Earl of Cork and Orrery. He spent many years studying chemistry at Oxford University. When Charles II decided to found the Royal Society, ever since the most distinguished scientific association in the world, Boyle was, together with Sir Christopher Wren (see page 88) and Samuel Pepys and others, a founder member.

Brunel, Isambard Kingdom (1806–1859), British engineer
If you go to Bristol you can see three very famous but quite different structures, the Clifton Suspension Bridge, the S.S. 'Great Britain', and Temple Meads Station. They were all designed by Isambard Kingdom Brunel, the greatest engineer of the 19th century – possibly of all time.

This remarkable man, son of a well-known engineer, Sir Marc

Brunel, was appointed engineer-in-chief of the Great Western Railway before he was thirty. Under his direction that splendid line was constructed, stretching from Paddington Station (which he designed) to Bristol, and also to Cornwall across the Saltash Bridge (which he also designed). Brunel also designed three famous ocean liners, the 'Great Western', the 'Great Britain' (the first ever to have a screw propeller) and the 'Great Eastern', for thirty years the largest vessel afloat anywhere in the world.

Brunel was a great friend of the engineer Robert Stephenson, son of George Stephenson (see page 80) and they died within weeks of each other, in 1859, both worn out by their energy and their hard work.

Brunelleschi, Filippo (1377–1446), Italian architect
In the 14th century there was in Europe a great revival of learning and a re-birth or Renaissance of art. This covered all

aspects of art, painting, sculpture, writing and architecture. Brunelleschi was one of the leading architects in this movement.

It was Brunelleschi who tried to get away from the familiar Gothic style of building so common in European churches and religious houses at the time. He preferred the style which the ancient Romans employed, and he longed to see it reintroduced all over Italy. So he adopted it in a variety of structures, churches, houses and public buildings. His greatest work was probably Florence Cathedral, to which he gave a huge dome.

Burghley, Lord, William Cecil, (1520–1598), English statesman
As a young official in the government of England, William Cecil had managed to adapt his political and religious views according to the temper of the reigning monarchs, Henry VIII, Edward VI and Mary I. In this time he mastered the arts of statecraft and foreign negotiation, and when Elizabeth I came to the throne in 1558 she did not hesitate to select him as her principal secretary of state.

For forty years this brilliant, painstaking, gentle-mannered and sometimes cunning man ran the government through some of its most dangerous times. He was the brains behind Elizabeth's middle-of-the-road religious settlement. He kept France and Spain from invading England. He encouraged trade, education and industry. And whenever the Queen was in trouble he always had an answer – except in the matter of her marriage.

This great man died in 1598, and left a son, Robert Cecil, who proved to be scarcely less brilliant than himself.

Burns, Robert (1759–1796), Scotland's national poet
'Robbie' Burns is the most famous name in Scottish poetry. He wrote, in a comparatively short life, a great volume of verse, some of it in the Scottish dialect. In his time he was as popular as his work is today.

Burns was really a farmer who educated himself at home. When his father died in 1784 Burns, with his brother and sisters, took a new farm at Mauchline, but while he was not afraid to work hard, he had no business head and it failed. At this time he began writing verse, and when he had some published in Edinburgh it was a great success, not least because it praised the virtues of the Scottish national character. As a result he was entertained everywhere.

Among his longer poems were 'The Cotter's Saturday Night' and 'Tam O' Shanter', which were not only stirring verses but also accurate pictures of the life of rich and poor in the Scotland of his time.

Burns wore himself out with work and with high living and died aged only thirty-six.

Caesar, Caius Julius (*c.* 100–44 BC), Roman dictator
'The noblest man that ever lived in the tide of times.' Thus did Shakespeare write of Julius Caesar, the great Roman dictator whose combination of talents has rarely been equalled in the history of the world. Command in battle, statecraft, oratory, authorship, the law, government of the Roman empire, friendship with his fellow men, he excelled in every field. He was witty, good-looking, kind, amazingly forgiving to his enemies, and he had immense will-power, great personal courage, and a complete freedom from fear of any kind.

The first forty years in Caesar's life were momentous for Rome. The republic was breaking down. Ambitious generals could threaten the city with armies and so choose their own officials and magistrates. Bribery and corruption were widespread. In these years Caesar achieved little beyond a magistracy or two and a medium command in Spain where he displayed bold leadership, courage and a willingness to share all hardships with his men. But he learned much; he acquired enough experience in the law courts to become the second greatest orator in Rome (see Cicero, page 28) and in the political clubs to become the most astute political manager.

Then in 60 BC he made a bid for real power. The two leading men

of Rome, Gn. Pompeius Magnus (Pompey), a successful general, and M. Licinius Crassus, a financier, were enemies. Caesar made them make friends and agree to rule Rome, with him, as a board of three. Then he was elected consul and in his year he introduced many important reforms. A year later he obtained his first big command, in Gaul.

For ten years he fought there, making two expeditions to Britain, and by 49 BC he had conquered and settled the whole country. He then wrote a history of his campaign, which has since been regarded as one of the finest works ever written by a Roman.

He came homewards to receive, as he expected, rewards for his men and honour for himself. Instead, he was declared a public enemy. So he marched on Rome, drove his jealous opponents out and had himself made dictator. For the next three years he fought his opponents in various parts of the empire and defeated them all, pardoning the survivors. By 45 BC he was master of the Roman world.

Among his more constructive acts were reforming the calendar, organising local government in the provinces, re-shaping Roman law, and enlarging the Senate so that a greater variety of people should have a say in Roman affairs.

In 44 BC he planned to set out to fight the great Parthian kingdom in the East which had been troubling Rome for some time. In the meanwhile, some senators, most of whom had been enemies and had been pardoned and owed everything to Caesar, plotted to murder him and restore the republic. And on 15th March, they cut him down and killed him, in the theatre of Pompey which was being used as a temporary Senate House.

But by murdering him they ensured that his ideas would live, for his great nephew Augustus (see page 11) completed the work that Julius Caesar had begun.

Canute (994–1035), king of Denmark, Norway, Sweden and England

Everybody knows that Canute sat on a throne by the sea's edge and ordered the waves to recede. What Canute in fact was doing was showing his flattering courtiers that he was not all-powerful. Of course the waves would not obey him.

Canute was one of the great rulers of the eleventh century. He was king of Denmark (and later of Norway and Sweden) when in 1016 his rival, Edmund Ironside, king of England, died. The English Council then elected Canute to succeed.

It was something of a gamble for up to then Canute had been heathen and ferocious. Now he changed. He became a Christian, taught himself law and statecraft, and began to rule his kingdoms well.

In England he insisted on having English advisers and courtiers, and with them he improved the nation's laws, encouraged trade and sponsored the development of schools.

Much of his time had to be spent in his other kingdoms, but Canute always said he was happiest in England.

Cartier, Jacques (1491–1557), French explorer
A landing in Canada had been made at the end of the 15th century by John and Sebastian Cabot, but they had no idea of the extent of Canada's size. It was Jacques Cartier, a French navigator, who undertook the first exploration into the interior of Canada. Between 1534 and 1541 he led three expeditions westwards to find a sea route to the east. On the first journey he discovered the Gulf of the St. Lawrence River. On the second he sailed up the river and reached what is now Montreal, but turned back because of severe weather and icy conditions.

In 1541 he made his last voyage to Canada, this time in search of minerals, but it was unproductive. Cartier made no attempt to build a settlement in Canada, and it was not until the early 17th century that this was done, by Champlain, another French explorer.

Caxton, William (*c.* 1422–1491), first English printer
Caxton started his working life in the silk business, in England and then in what is now Belgium. He made a success of it and then decided to travel in Europe. On a visit to Cologne he saw a printing press, one of the first ever to be made in Europe. It interested him enormously and he began to learn all about printing.

In 1476 he brought a press over to England and at Westminster he set up the first printing business in the country. There, over the next fifteen years he printed nearly a hundred books. These included *The Dictes and Sayings of the Philosophers, The Mirror of the World,* and Chaucer's *Canterbury Tales.*

Caxton's press contributed enormously to the spread of learning. Soon, books no longer had to be copied out laboriously by hand, and there were more books for more people to read.

Cervantes, Miguel de (1547–1616), Spanish writer
Cervantes is probably Spain's most famous author, and yet he

wrote little more than one book, *Don Quixote*, which became one of the best-known novels of all times. It is a satire on the romantic tales of chivalry which were then very fashionable. Don Quixote rides about on a grand horse, carrying a lance, followed by his squire, Sancho Panza, a real figure of fun.

Cervantes was a soldier who fought at the battle of Lepanto in 1571 where he lost an arm. During a skirmish a few years later between Spanish ships and Barbary pirates, he was captured and spent some years as their prisoner. Returning home five years later, he went into business as a wheat merchant and over the next fifteen years or so he made a lot of money.

He began to write *Don Quixote* in about 1605 but did not finish the second volume until a year before his death.

Charlemagne (742–814), first emperor of the Holy Roman Empire. Charles the Great, or Charlemagne, became king of the Franks in 771. His principal advantages were an ability to wield a sword better than most men and great personal bravery. Otherwise, he was almost completely uneducated and had to learn about kingship the hard way.

Soon after his accession he set out to unite as much of Western Europe as he could under his crown, and he began by conquering large tracts of Italy, then held by the Lombards. By 800 he was master of Central and Western Europe, and the Pope crowned him first emperor of the Holy Roman Empire, as he was also the champion of the Church of Rome.

Charlemagne encouraged learning on a wide scale, founded universities, patronised scholars (including Welsh, Irish and English ones), and fostered the arts. He promoted building programmes, created alliances with foreign kings, including Offa of Mercia in England, and successfully staved off some very fierce Viking attacks.

This great ruler died in 814.

Chaucer, Geoffrey (*c.* 1340–1400), English poet

Geoffrey Chaucer was the son of a London vintner who did business with the Royal Family. When he was a boy Chaucer managed to get appointed as a page to the king, Edward III, and thereafter for the rest of his life he was employed from time to time in various capacities, such as ambassador or customs controller, by the Royal Family, especially by John of Gaunt, Edward III's fourth son.

From quite an early age Chaucer also wrote poetry. Then in 1373 he embarked on a big project, *The Canterbury Tales*, by which he became famous in his own time and which today ranks among the greatest works of all literature.

More than twenty stories are interspersed with conversation pieces. They are imaginary tales told by a company of pilgrims on their way from London to Canterbury. They are still fresh, funny, sometimes naughty; and never dull.

Chopin, Frederic (1810–1849), Polish composer

Chopin, who was born near Warsaw, was another great musician who showed brilliance at a very early age. He was playing the piano in public long before he was ten, by which time he had also composed some of his shorter pieces. When he was eighteen he left Poland and settled in Paris where he met, and worked with, many distinguished musicians, including Mendelssohn and Liszt.

Chopin, who did write some orchestral music, concentrated on piano pieces, and many of these are brilliant in their structure and superbly melodic. The 'Raindrop Prelude', 'Tristesse', the 'Revolutionary Study', and the 'Scherzo in C Sharp minor', are but a few of his works which are still played and enjoyed all over the world. His work, however, led him to neglect his health, and he caught tuberculosis. For some years he was looked after by the novelist Georges Sand, but she made so many demands on his emotional strength that he got worse. A heavy tour giving recitals in Europe ruined his health completely and he died in 1849.

Churchill, Sir Winston (1874–1965), British statesman, soldier, author

In the summer of 1940 all Western Europe lay in the grip of Nazi Germany and the most powerful army of the world stood poised to invade the British Isles. Churchill was appointed prime minister at this critical time, and by his stirring inspiration, his speeches which roused the British against the Germans, and his handling of the nation's war effort, he made the Germans think again, and in the autumn they called the invasion off.

It was the first set-back to Hitler's otherwise invincible progress through Europe (see page 50) and it gave tremendous hope and encouragement to all the oppressed nations. Five years later, Western Europe was liberated by British and American forces. Churchill had seen the British people through to victory.

This 'many-sided genius' was the descendant of the great Duke of Marlborough (see page 62). His young life was full of adventure. He fought in Cuba, took part in the charge of the 21st Lancers at Omdurman in 1898, and, as a war correspondent in the South African War, was captured by Boer troops, but escaped. In 1900 he entered Parliament as Conservative MP for Oldham, changing sides to the Liberals in 1904. He played a big part in pushing through many important reforms, including national insurance, labour exchanges, and reform of the House of Lords.

In the First World War he was First Lord of the Admiralty and he reorganised the Navy. But he was blamed for the failure of the Dardanelles campaign and for a while his political career was at an end. He went to the front line in France. In 1917 he was recalled to office and became combined Air and War Minister. In 1924 he returned to Parliament as a Conservative but he was unpopular with his colleagues over many things, including British policy in India. For some years he was a back-bencher. Many said he was finished. During this time he wrote many books, including a biography of Marlborough, and he also painted some vigorous and colourful pictures.

When Great Britain went to war with Hitler in 1939, Churchill

was brought back to office as First Lord of the Admiralty, and again he organised the Navy so that it could play its vital role. Then, when the prime minister, Chamberlain, resigned in May 1940 following criticism of his war policy, Churchill succeeded.

After the war, Churchill was in opposition for six years, and he wrote his history of the Second World War, in six volumes, which won for him the Nobel Prize for Literature. He became prime minister again in 1951 and governed for four years. Then he retired, wrote more books and painted more pictures, and generally enjoyed the rest he had more than deserved after sixty years of service to his country. Churchill died in 1965, aged 90, and was given a splendid state funeral. He was mourned by millions all over the world. Rightly, he has been called the greatest Englishman of all time.

Cicero, Marcus Tullius (106–43 BC), Roman statesman and orator. Cicero was one of those tragic figures of history whose lives, despite certain successes, were overall failures. Born in humble circumstances in northern Italy, Cicero received a fine education in which he showed astonishing power as an orator. In his time he was to write and deliver some of the greatest speeches in history.

Cicero managed through hard work to get to a position where he could stand for consul, and in 64 BC he was elected. In his year of office, 63 BC, he crushed a revolt against the state led by a bankrupt and discontented nobleman, L. Sergius Catilina, but unfortunately he believed the revolt – and the suppression of it – to be more important than it really was, and he never stopped boasting about how he 'saved the state'.

When Julius Caesar (see page 20) and Pompey went to war in 49 BC, Cicero took Pompey's side. Caesar, the victor, pardoned him and even sought his advice, but after the murder of Caesar, Cicero made a speech saying it was a glorious deed, which, of course, it was not. Caesar's heir, Octavian (see Augustus, page 11) was not so forgiving and he had Cicero put to death, in 43 BC.

Collins, Michael (1890–1922), Irish patriot
Michael Collins is widely regarded in Ireland as the greatest Irishman since king Brian Boru (926–1014). Born and educated in Cork, he spent ten years in England as a civil servant. In 1916, hearing that Irish patriots were going to rise up against their English masters and declare a republic, he rushed back to Dublin to join them. The rebellion was a failure, however, and Collins was imprisoned.

When he was released he set to work to reconstruct the resistance organisation, and in three years (1918–21) he and his agents so completely disrupted the English administration that the government agreed to discuss terms. Some rebels wanted a full republic; Collins and his supporters were willing to accept a Free State, that is, the sort of independence Canada had, and this was agreed.

Almost at once civil war broke out between the supporters of the Free State and Republicans and though the Free State supporters won, Michael Collins was assassinated.

Columbus, Christopher (1451–1506), Italian born navigator
Christopher Columbus, a brave, determined, and on the whole unhappy man, was an Italian navigator who was born at Genoa. In the 1480s when Portuguese navigators were making voyages towards South Africa looking for a sea route to India and China, Columbus tried to get the Portuguese and the Spanish kings to back a voyage westwards, which he believed fervently would be more fruitful.

Finally, in 1492, the Spanish king and queen, Ferdinand and Isabella, grudgingly offered support, and on 3rd August he set sail in the Santa Maria, accompanied by two boats, the Pinta and the Nina. Nine weeks later, on 11th October, he sighted land, and a day

later his ships dropped anchor close by. Columbus stepped ashore from a row-boat and fell on his knees, praising God and thanking Him for allowing him to discover the western route to China.

In fact, Columbus had not reached China at all, but had landed on one of the islands later to be grouped as the Bahamas. He had discovered a new world, however, one which other Spanish and Portuguese navigators were quick to explore.

Columbus returned to Europe and proclaimed his discovery. Then he made several more voyages to the West Indian islands and touched the mainland of both North and South America. But he had provoked much jealousy among other navigators and officials and they kept bringing charges against him of corrupt dealings with the natives. On one occasion he was arrested and sent home to Spain in chains. The king released him but would not restore his honours.

Tragically, Columbus died in great poverty and misery.

Constantine I, (AD 280–337), Roman emperor
Flavius Valerius Aurelius Constantinus was the son of one of Diocletian's Caesars, Constantius, and he spent his earlier years in military service. When Diocletian resigned as head of the board of emperors (see page 38) and Maximian had to resign as co-emperor at the same time, Constantius became emperor in the west and Constantine was declared Caesar. His father died soon afterwards and Constantine, who had never approved of Diocletian's idea of the board of emperors, set out to get rid of his rivals and rule alone. By 324 he had succeeded when the last, Licinius, was defeated in battle and executed.

Constantine then decided that the capital of the Roman empire would be better placed further in the East and in 324 he laid the foundation stone of a splendid new city at Byzantium, a small town on the edge of east Europe, overlooking the Bosphorus. Six years later the city was built and he dedicated it to God at a great ceremony. In 335 he divided the empire between his three sons and two nephews but retained overall control. But, when Constantine died in 337 civil war broke out almost at once among his sons, destroying much he had done.

Cook, Captain James (1728–1779), English explorer
Perhaps the greatest of all English navigators was James Cook. He sailed round New Zealand in 1770–71 and charted it. He returned home via Australia and charted the unknown east coast thus revealing to the British public the existence of a whole new land to which, before long, people began to emigrate.

Soon after Cook returned from this voyage, he was sent out to search for a vast continent which many scientists believed was beyond Australia. For three years he searched in vain, because of course it was not there, but in the effort he discovered fresh lands, including New Caledonia.

In 1776 Cook set out on his last voyage to find a route north of North America, from Pacific to Atlantic. He charted the Pacific coast right up to the Bering Strait but did not find the route. So he turned southwards and discovered the Hawaiian islands. There Cook was murdered by Hawaiians who misunderstood his motives and thought he had come to kill them.

Copernicus, Nicolaus (1473–1543), Polish astronomer
Nikolaj Kopernik, better known to history as Nicolaus Copernicus, was a Polish astronomer who put forward the theory that the earth and the planets revolve around the sun. This may not seem so startling an idea now, but in those days men were accustomed to believing that the earth was flat and that the sun moved around it, and in many countries it was a serious offence to say otherwise.

Copernicus, who studied astronomy, theology and medicine at the university of Cracow, and taught for many years in Italy, did not publish his theory until just before his death in 1543.

Cortez, Hernan (1485–1547), Spanish conqueror of Mexico
One of the most tragic acts in history was the destruction by the Spaniards led by Hernan Cortez of the ancient civilisation of the Aztecs in Mexico.

Cortez, son of a Spanish nobleman, went to the West Indies in the early 16th century in search of adventure. In 1518, the Spanish governor of Cuba, Narvaez, sent him with a small force, armed with muskets and equipped with horses, to explore the mainland of Mexico. There, in 1519, Cortez erected a settlement on the coast and called it Vera Cruz.

When he came upon the Aztecs, an ancient and splendid civilised people who dominated Mexico and Central America, he bargained with them and then treacherously turned on them. He captured their king, Montezuma, and destroyed his great capital, Mexico City. Then he systematically dismantled the whole apparatus of Aztec government and put many of the people to death. Many more were put into slavery.

What enabled the Spaniards to overturn the Aztecs so easily was the fact that they had horses and guns, neither of which the Aztecs had ever seen, or for that matter, ever needed.

Cromwell, Oliver (1599–1658), English statesman, soldier and Lord Protector
For more than a century after his death in 1658, Cromwell was regarded with hate and revulsion, chiefly because he was responsible for the execution of the king, Charles I, in 1649, after the Civil War. Then, men began to think again, study his speeches, his acts of parliament, and his military deeds, and they found him to have been a great Englishman, a view shared by many people of his own time.

This robust, cheerful, brave and devout Huntingdonshire-born country gentleman entered parliament in 1628. The next year the king dissolved parliament and ruled alone for eleven years. But he ruled so badly that he had to call a new parliament in 1640. The members, one of whom was Cromwell, were very angry men. But

the king still would not mend his ways, and in 1642 civil war broke out.

Aged nearly fifty, Cromwell displayed the most amazing gifts as a general, a strategist, and a leader of men, in several battles, all of which he won. After parliament had defeated the king and imprisoned him, Cromwell tried to persuade him to rule properly. Instead, the king secretly tried to raise aid from abroad to restore him to full power, and when parliament discovered this they put him on trial. He was found guilty of treason and he was executed. These were hard times.

For a few years no one emerged as head of state though Cromwell was the strongest and most respected man in the country because of his great military prestige. In 1653 he had himself made Lord Protector with the help of his friends. Over the next five years he achieved much. He reformed the courts of justice and the system of taxation, and he granted freedom of belief to all kinds of Protestants. Abroad he raised English prestige so high that European leaders asked him to arbitrate in their disputes. He also laid the foundations of the British Empire by encouraging exploration and colonial settlement in the West Indies and America.

Cromwell died in 1658. He was not greatly mourned, for he had been ahead of his time in his ideas of government and he had had to act harshly on several occasions. But when the monarchy was restored in 1660 it was never quite the same.

Da Gama, Vasco (c. 1469–1524), Portuguese explorer
It has been said that Vasco da Gama was, more than anyone else, responsible for the prosperity that the Portuguese have had since 1500. This brave and imaginative sailor was sent by the Portuguese king, Emanuel I, in 1497 to go round the Cape of South Africa and find a sea route to India. With four small ships da Gama left Lisbon in July and rounded the Cape of Good Hope towards the end of the year.

Then he sailed up the east coast to Malindi where he persuaded some Arab pilots to lead him to the west coast of India. He reached Calicut on 19th May, 1498, thereby completing the first voyage from Europe round Africa to the East. He came home, and when he reached Lisbon in 1499 he received a splendid welcome from the king and his subjects. Now Portugal could trade directly with the East without having to pay costly taxes to the various countries through which their goods-laden caravans, on the land routes, had to pass to get to Europe.

Darius I (c. 558–486 BC), king of Persia
'King of Kings, King of land peopled by all races, for long King of this Great Earth.' Thus runs an inscription in rock in Persia, and it describes how Darius the Great saw himself when king of Persia from 521 to 486 BC.

This splendid ruler, son-in-law of Cyrus the Great, founder of the Persian empire (whose 2500th anniversary was celebrated with great pomp in Iran in October 1971) devoted his reign to expanding Persian territory and to beautifying Persian cities. He built a new capital at Persepolis, which had a vast fortress on a site five thousand feet high. He constructed a grand trunk road from Susa to Ephesus, called the King's Highway, which could be covered by a fast rider in six days although it was over a thousand miles long. And he introduced a postal system which used this road for swift delivery.

Darius also reorganised the administration of Persia and of the lands he conquered. He divided the empire into twenty provinces and put a locally born official in charge of each.

His career, though a splendid one, was not without disappointments. He failed to crush Greek independence and lost a critical battle at Marathon in 490 BC which ensured their freedom.

Darwin, Charles (1809–1882), British naturalist
Until the middle of the last century most people believed the Bible story that Adam and Eve were the first people on earth. They had no knowledge of prehistoric man and would not have accepted for a moment that there was any relationship between man and monkeys.

Charles Darwin, a Cambridge educated botanist, changed all that. In 1859 he published his book *On the Origin of Species* and it was a sensation. In it he showed that man and monkeys were both descended from an earlier ancestor which vaguely resembled a cross between the two. And that ancestor lived hundreds of thousands of years ago. He based his theory on the development of the animals he saw on the Galapagos Islands which he had visited on a scientific voyage of discovery.

This enraged the high-minded Christian Victorians as it dismissed the Bible's Creation story. For some time Darwin was subjected to much public ridicule, though forward-thinking scientists admired him for his boldness and for the brilliance of his research. He seems to have been forgiven, however, by the public and he was buried in Westminster Abbey.

Da Vinci, Leonardo (1452–1519), Italian artist and scientific genius

This amazing son of an Italian lawyer has been described as a universal genius. He excelled as a painter, sculptor, architect, inventor, musician, mathematician, engineer, anatomist and naturalist, and doubtless would have dominated many other careers if he had had the time.

Leonardo was years ahead of his contemporaries in many fields. In science he disregarded what had been written or done before and accepted only what he could observe or test for himself. This is the true way to do research. In painting he experimented with new materials and he produced some of the most beautiful works of all time, notably, 'The Last Supper', and 'The Mona Lisa'. The latter was the first portrait showing the model in a relaxed position and it heralded a new style of portrait painting.

Leonardo was fascinated by nature. He drew animals, fishes and birds, and he studied their movements. As he was also a skilled

36

engineer he considered ways of imitating these natural movements like flight, and thus gave birth to the idea of aeroplanes, submarines, etc.

Unfortunately, it seems that even in the 16th century, an age of great artistic and scientific achievement in Europe, men could not reach up to his level of thought, and many of his ideas died with him and had to be thought up again by other people in later generations.

Davy, Sir Humphrey (1778–1829), British chemist

Davy was a Cornishman who by his brilliance as an experimental chemist won himself the envied position of Professor of Chemistry at the Royal Institution in London, at the early age of twenty-four. In a very full and interesting life he made a number of discoveries, including the elements sodium and potassium, and the fact that diamonds are a form of carbon. He also invented a safety lamp for coal miners that was named after him. The Davy Lamp was used for years, until towards the end of the nineteenth century, when reliable electric light was introduced in mines.

Davy was made a baronet in 1818, and two years later he was elected President of the Royal Society, the foremost position in the British world of science.

Diaz, Bartholomew (c. 1450–1500), Portuguese explorer

The second half of the 15th century was one of great activity in the field of exploration, especially among Portuguese navigators. The principal goal was a sea route to India round Africa. In 1486 a Portuguese captain, Bartholomew Diaz, was sent by King John II to try to get further south than earlier navigators. In 1488 he rounded the southern tip of Africa but turned back because of severe storms, passing the cape which he called the Cape of Storms.

Arriving home in 1489 he reported to the king who said 'Call it not the Cape of Storms, but the Cape of Good Hope!' It was an important voyage as it opened the way for Vasco da Gama (see page 34) whom Diaz accompanied for part of the distance on the voyage of 1497–9.

Dickens, Charles (1812–1870), English novelist
Charles Dickens was one of the greatest of all English novelists. His books were widely read for their humour, their wonderful descriptiveness, their amazing character creations, and their vivid dialogue. Many of them were also important documents of life as it was in his youth, times which were, for all but the aristocratic and the rich, very unhappy. It was an age of brutal schools, of long hours for very small pay in badly lit factories or in dangerous mines, when workers lived perpetually in debt in mean little houses grouped in endless rows in the most unattractive parts of the country.

Dickens himself had had the poorest of childhoods, so bad that his parents spent many months in prison for debt and he was utterly neglected. He was indeed well qualified to write about social evils and parts of his book *David Copperfield* are thought to be autobiographical.

As a child he worked in a blacking factory labelling the pots and later became a clerk. Finally he was accepted as a newspaper reporter and began to write sketches for magazines using the pen-name 'Boz'. This led to him writing a series of articles called *The Pickwick Papers* which made him famous. Among his best-known books are *Oliver Twist*, *Great Expectations*, and *A Tale of Two Cities*. Some of his works were instrumental in getting reforms carried out in working conditions.

Diocletian (245–313), Roman emperor
Gaius Aurelius Valerius Diocletianus began life in the most humble way. His father is believed to have been a freed slave from Dalmatia (now Yugoslavia) and young Diocletian worked his way up the ranks of the army with great speed. When in 284 the last of a succession of emperors, most of them weak-willed and unable to

provide firm government, died, the troops of the imperial armies elected Diocletian, believing he would give the empire the order it needed.

And so he did. At once he realised that the empire was too big to be ruled by one man. So he appointed himself and Maximian, a close friend, with two deputies, called Caesars, who were Constantius and Galerius, to form a board of emperors to rule over about a quarter of the empire, each with a separate capital.

For twenty years they ruled, for the most part well. Many reforms were introduced in the law, in the army and in government. They even tried to regulate prices to control profiteering by traders.

Then, in 305 Diocletian suddenly decided to resign and grow vegetables on his private estate in Dalmatia where, eight years later, he died.

Drake, Sir Francis (c. 1540–1596), English admiral
It is doubtful whether Drake actually played bowls on Plymouth Hoe as the Spanish Armada sailed up the English Channel. But the story is a good illustration of the extraordinary courage and coolness which this Devonshire-born sea captain displayed on numerous occasions in his life.

For years Drake raided well-armed and heavily laden Spanish treasure ships in West Indian and Atlantic waters. Then in 1577 he set out on a voyage to attack the Spanish on the Pacific side of South America, and in doing this he also sailed right round the world, the first captain to do so (see Magellan on page 60). When he returned to Plymouth in 1580, Queen Elizabeth I knighted him on board his ship.

Drake was second in command of the English naval forces which scattered the ships of the Spanish Armada in 1588, and it was really his plan of letting loose small fireships among the big Spanish galleons that turned a defeat into a rout.

Drake died in 1596 on yet another raiding expedition.

Edison, Thomas Alva (1847–1931), American inventor
Edison is probably the best-known name in American science and engineering. He is credited with hundreds of inventions, and he certainly took out many patents in his time. He was associated with the electric light bulb, he invented railway signals, the gramophone (which he called a phonograph), storage batteries and many other popular household things. This is all the more remarkable because he left school at eleven, and practically all of his knowledge was acquired by reading in his spare time while doing a succession of menial jobs, such as a newspaper round.

Eisenhower, General Dwight David (1890–1969), American president and military leader
General Eisenhower, known to his American admirers as 'Ike', was a professional soldier who in 1942 was picked by President Roosevelt to command American forces in Europe. He had not held

any big command before but he was an extremely good manager of men and it was thought by the Allied Heads of State, that is Roosevelt and Churchill, that he would be the best person to bring together military commanders of the many nations fighting Germany. And so it proved. Under his leadership the Allies drove the German occupying forces out of all European countries in the West and compelled them to surrender.

Eisenhower stayed in Europe to command the Allied forces controlling the Germans, and then he returned to America in 1945. In 1952 he was elected president of the United States. As a politician, however, he was by no means as successful, though he was re-elected in 1956, largely on the strength of his great military prestige.

Erasmus, Desiderius (*c.* 1466–1536), Dutch scholar
Erasmus, whose real name was Geert Geerts, entered a monastery when he was a boy, but before long he found the life was not stimulating enough for his undoubtedly high intellect. He left and went to the university of Paris to study theology and classics. He soon made his mark, first as a brilliant pupil and then as a teacher.

Even the famous intellectual life in Paris began to bore him and he moved on, never again settling anywhere for long. He became a kind of travelling scholar, enriching every learned society or university he visited, including Oxford and Cambridge where he was very happy. At Cambridge he actually held a professorship of divinity.

Erasmus wrote many books, taking advantage of the newly introduced process of printing. Some of these were about religion, questioning the way the church administered it, and opening people's minds to doubt. All the same, he never joined the reformers Luther (see page 59) and Calvin. As he said, 'I will not give up Rome until I find something better.'

Ericsson, Leif (11th century), Norwegian explorer

Ericsson was the son of Eric the Red, the Norwegian Viking chief who founded a colony in Iceland and also discovered the south-west corner of Greenland.

Ericsson inherited his father's lust for adventure and discovery – and also his ability to win the hearts of men. In about 1004, having spent some years in the Viking colony in Greenland, he set out to explore the west coast of Greenland. But the winds took him out to sea and for days his long ship with its high prow was battered by the Atlantic. Finally, when the wind dropped, he sighted land and steered towards it. Landing, his crew scrambled across the sand and found wild vine bushes growing. They called the land Vinland. It was in fact America. Without realising it they had anticipated Columbus by nearly 500 years.

Euclid (*c.* 350–*c.* 300 BC), Greek mathematician

If you like mathematics at school, you can be grateful to Euclid, for it was this Greek mathematician, living in Alexandria, who worked out most of the theorems. These were put together in a work called the *Elements of Geometry*, in about 320 BC. It may well have been a text book for students of mathematics at the college in Alexandria in which he taught which had recently been founded by Alexander the Great (see page 7).

Fleming, Sir Alexander (1881–1955), Scottish scientist

If you cut your finger and get an infection as a result, your doctor will give you some penicillin, or a similar drug, as a matter of course, and the infection will be cured, probably very quickly.

It was not so thirty or more years ago, when infection was much harder to fight. What changed this was the discovery of penicillin, a mould or fungus which has germ-killing qualities. And the man who found it was the Scottish bacteriologist, Alexander Fleming, a quiet, unassuming professor at St. Mary's Hospital in London.

Fleming first discovered the mould in 1928, but it required several more years of research and development to make it possible to apply it on a wide scale and so save lives in all parts of the world. It is pleasant to think that Fleming, unlike some medical benefactors, was rewarded and honoured widely in his lifetime.

Franklin, Benjamin (1706–1790), American statesman and scientist

Franklin was an American scientist who invented the lightning conductor and did some early experiments with electricity. He was also a very able statesman who played a big part in the foundation of the United States republic.

Born in Boston of very humble parents, Benjamin Franklin was almost entirely self-taught, as from an early age he had to go out to work. He was for a time a printer, and this gave him the chance to publish his own newspaper, the *Pennsylvania Gazette*, which became very influential. At this time he also began his experiments in physical science, and he looked into many things such as meteorology, oceanography and agriculture.

By 1775 Franklin's reputation was so great that he was asked to assist in drafting the Declaration of Independence, along with Jefferson (see page 52) and in framing the Constitution of the United States which followed in 1787.

Galileo (1564–1642), Italian astronomer and physicist

In about 1582, Galileo Galilei, a young student in Pisa, sat watching a candelabrum in Pisa cathedral swing on a rope. After a while he noticed that the swing from left to right took the same time to complete although the distance of swing was shortening. He had discovered that pendulum movement produces a regular time measurement, and the pendulum clock was eventually developed from this observation.

Galileo, as he was called, became professor of mathematics at Padna

university in 1593, and in this post he put forward a number of startling theories. He showed that bodies of different weight fall to the ground at the same speed in vacuum. He invented the astronomical telescope and with it proved that the theory of Copernicus (see page 31), that the earth moves round the sun, was correct. He also invented an air thermometer.

Galileo got into much trouble for his ideas, especially for proving Copernicus' theory, and more than once he was compelled to withdraw his propositions, which he did in the interests of science, so that he could go on working. Otherwise, he might have been put to death.

This great man, who was kind and considerate, went blind in about 1535 and his last years were not happy ones.

Garibaldi, Giuseppe (1807–1882), Italian patriot
In the middle of the 19th century patriots in some of the Italian

states which had been ruled for a long time by other European powers like Austria and Spain, decided to unite to form a new nation. But it was not easy because many of the heads of state were opposed to unity. Among them were the rulers of Sicily and Naples.

In about 1860 Giuseppe Garibaldi, an army officer from Piedmont, one of the states that did want unity, and a man of great bravery and leadership, formed an army of about 1000 men, tough and ready to fight, and dressed them in red shirts. Then he invaded Sicily and in a short time won it. From there he invaded Naples and drove the king out.

He then retired to his estate but returned to politics and was elected deputy in 1861. On the outbreak of war in 1864 he assumed command of a volunteer army to fight for Italian unity. Final unity of all Italy was not achieved until 1870, and Garibaldi was elected a representative for Rome in the Italian Parliament of 1874.

Genghiz Khan (1162–1227). Mongol conqueror
Genghiz Khan, even as a boy in Mongolia, had dreams of world conquest. When his father, a powerful chief, died in 1175, young Temujine, as his real name was, succeeded him and began to build up a tough fighting force which he trained and disciplined with great thoroughness. Sometime towards the end of the 12th century his warriors, almost all marvellous horsemen, gave Temujine the title Genghiz Khan, which means something like 'Lord Absolute'.

In about 1206 Genghiz was ready to march, and he attacked China. He breached the famous Great Wall in three places and soon all northern China was in his hands. Then he turned westwards and overran parts of India, Persia, Afghanistan, and even took large districts of Russia. By 1225 he was master of nearly all Asia. He said it would have taken him a year to cross it from one end to the other.

Genghiz, who was by no means as savage as one might suppose, had great plans for administering his new territory, but he died before he could get these put into action.

Glyndŵr, Owain (*c.* 1359–*c.* 1416), Welsh national leader
The Welsh nation was crushed by Edward I of England in 1282, and incorporated in his kingdom. But the national spirit was not quenched, and one hundred and twenty years later the Welsh in the north rose in rebellion against England. They were led by the bold and fiery Owain Glyndŵr, himself a descendant of the last independent prince of Wales. For years Owain successfully raided English border counties like Shropshire and Cheshire and defeated all English armies sent against him. He even summoned a Parliament at Machynlleth and declared Wales an independent sovereign state.

Then, suddenly, he vanished, and with him went the urge to resist English rule. The Welsh have still not obtained their independence but they have their ancient language and culture.

Greco, El (1546–1614), Spanish painter
El Greco was the name given by the Spanish to a Cretan-born painter, Domenikos Theotokopoulos, who went to live and work in Spain. He studied art in Venice under Titian and it is not known for certain why he left Italy for Spain and when questioned later he refused to say.

He settled in Toledo and over the next years he produced many fine pictures, chiefly for churches and monasteries. One of these was 'The Burial of the Count of Orgaz'. Greco used contrasting colours to great effect to heighten the dramatic nature of his pictures. His style was very individual and is instantly recognisable.

Gutenburg, Johann (*c.* 1400–*c.* 1468), German printer
Gutenburg is credited with having invented printing from movable type. He certainly introduced the idea into Europe. The Chinese had already developed movable type printing several hundred years earlier but their invention had not spread to Europe, and Gutenburg is said not to have known of their achievement.

His first successful press was working in about 1430. It has been difficult to say which, if any, books were printed by him, but the Gutenburg Bible, discovered in a famous library in France in 1760, is believed to have been one of the first works to come off an early press. A fragment of an astronomical calendar, discovered in 1901, is also said to have come from a book printed by him.

Hammurabi (18th century BC), Babylonian king and lawgiver
The very first code of law, or list of rules on how to behave, was written down by Hammurabi. He was king of the ancient kingdom of Babylon for forty years.

Hammurabi's laws may not seem perhaps as reasonable as ours today, but it was a very important step to get them written down. It ensured that society had some degree of order which is essential if it is to survive. One rule stated that theft from a noble should be repaid thirty times over but theft from a commoner only ten times. Another said that if a house collapsed and killed the owner, the builder was to be put to death; if the house killed the owner's son, the builder's son was to die.

Hammurabi was also a conqueror, and in his time he made the kingdom of Babylon one of the most powerful in the known world. This is what he said of himself: 'I made an end of war. I promised the welfare of the land. I have governed the people in peace. I have sheltered them in my strength'.

Hannibal (*c.* 247–183 BC), Carthaginian military leader
Anyone who brought an army of infantry and cavalry, accompanied by a herd of elephants, across the Alps into Italy would earn his place in history. Hannibal, son of the Carthaginian general, Hamilcar Barca, did very much more than that.

Hannibal was, as a boy, made by his father to swear an oath that he would fight the Romans whenever he could. In 221 BC, when only twenty-six, he was appointed commander of the Carthaginian forces which occupied southern Spain. He began operations against

the Romans in the northern part by capturing one of their towns, Saguntum. Then he took his army across the Alps, with about fifty elephants, and made for the Italian plains.

The Alpine crossing was disastrous. All the elephants and many thousands of men and horses were killed. But Hannibal was not deterred, and with the remains of his army he charged down into Italy and defeated every army the Romans sent against him, at the Ticinus, the Trebia and Lake Trasimene. He then marched down the peninsula and was about to threaten Rome itself when he changed direction and headed for the east coast. At Cannae in 216 BC he inflicted the greatest defeat ever sustained by Rome in all its twelve centuries. Eighty thousand cavalry and infantry were killed or captured. Had Hannibal moved against Rome he could have taken the city with ease. But again he held his hand – we know not why.

Instead, he wasted valuable time in small campaigns in Italy which though usually successful were not productive. In 203 BC his home government recalled him to go to Africa where a year later the final battle between him and Rome was fought at Zama. The Roman commander, Publius Cornelius Scipio, proved to be his equal and he overcame the great Carthaginian.

Hannibal's last years were spent intriguing against Rome in various parts of the world, but to no avail, and in 183 BC he committed suicide.

Henry the Navigator (1394–1460), Portuguese prince and patron of explorers
Prince Henry, known to history as 'The Navigator' because of his encouragement and financing of explorers, was the third son of king John I of Portugal. After a few years in military service, he retired to a large mansion at Sagres, on Cape St. Vincent, and there set up a kind of school for navigators and explorers. It was an age when men were beginning to throw off their fears of what happened beyond the horizon at sea. Once they thought they would fall off the globe, but now they wanted to find out what really happened. They were also anxious to find a sea route to India and China.

Henry employed the best geographers and astronomers he could find and he equipped the school with the latest scientific instruments. In 1433 the first breakthrough came when he sent Gil Eannes out to sea and this brave captain rounded Cape Bojador and sailed on to the Gulf of Guinea which, contrary to popular belief, was not a sea of flames. Other voyages followed until Bartholomew Diaz (see page 37) rounded the Cape of Good Hope and thus made da Gama's voyage to India possible (see page 34).

But Henry had died before these last achievements.

Herodotus (c. 480–c. 425 BC), Greek historian
Herodotus was a Greek traveller who has come to be known as the father of history. This really means he was the first person to write historical accounts of events without over-glamorising them

or dressing them up with superstition or mythology. In his time he travelled over most of the world then known to the Greeks.

When he finally settled in Italy, at the Greek colony of Thurii, he sat down to write his nine volume history of the Greco-Persian wars, from about 500 to about 480 BC. From these we know the details of the battle of Marathon, 490 BC and the exploits of Themistocles (see page 82).

But these books tell of more than just the wars. They include the observations he made on his travels, and by so doing give the whole period something of its real character.

Hitler, Adolf (1889–1945), German dictator

Adolf Hitler was Führer (leader) of the German state from 1933 to 1945. In that time he ruled with absolute power and his people, who treated him more as a god, did almost whatever he asked of them. His policies plunged the world into a war in which nearly fifty million people died.

Born in Austria, Hitler was an impoverished art student in Vienna when the First World War broke out in 1914. He volunteered for the army and had a creditable career as a corporal, winning the Iron Cross for bravery. When the Germans and Austrians were defeated in 1918, he, like millions of other troops, was unemployed and had nothing to do but brood. Hitler began thinking about the causes of the defeat and soon decided that it was a combination of corruption in high places, Jewish influence, and Communist plotting. So he formed a new political party that would bring Germany back to greatness, avenge the defeat, and provide work for the people. It was called the National Socialist German Workers Party, known thereafter as the Nazi party for short.

To begin with, the party grew slowly, but as the unemployment figures went up, so did the membership, because none of the other parties or leaders in power seemed able to do anything about it. Hitler appealed to the worst qualities of the German people, brutality and blind obedience to one's superiors, and by violent

methods, like organised riots, bullied his way into power in 1933 when the President, von Hindenburg, appointed him Chancellor. When Hindenburg died the next year, Hitler assumed the presidency and called himself Führer.

Hitler and his henchmen then set out on a course of political bullying and where that failed, military conquest, which by 1942 had made him master of nearly all Europe including millions of square miles of Russia. But this had involved him in war with Great Britain, the United States and many other countries. The combined forces of these nations gradually wore the Nazi military machine down and in 1945 Hitler committed suicide as Russian guns shelled his palace in Berlin. The Germans then surrendered.

This man, who had been responsible for the murder of over six million Jews bringing more misery on mankind than any ruler, before or since, was a vegetarian, did not smoke or drink and was kind to children and animals. It was an amazing contrast.

Hudson, Henry (*c.* 1550–1611), English explorer

Hudson's Bay in Canada is a huge inland sea, nearly half a million square miles in area. It is named after the English navigator, Henry Hudson, who in 1609, with financial help from the Dutch East India Company set out to look for a north-west passage to the Far East, north of Canada. Hudson did not find the passage, but he did discover this bay.

On his way back, some of his crew mutinied and turned him and several officers out in an open boat. Hudson and his companions were never seen again.

Jefferson, Thomas (1743–1826), American president

'. . . All men are created equal, that they are endowed by their Creator with certain unalienable rights, that among these are life, liberty and the pursuit of happiness.'

One of the most famous declarations in history, this phrasing is part of the Declaration of Independence issued by the American colonists in 1776 during their war against British dominion. It was written by the ablest statesman among them, Thomas Jefferson, a Virginian lawyer.

This brilliant man was governor of Virginia during the war. When the fighting stopped and the colonists won their freedom, Jefferson was sent to France as the first ambassador of the new republic. There he gave the French intellectuals who were behind the French Revolution the benefit of his experience and skill in words for their Declaration of the Rights of Man.

Jefferson was elected president of the United States in 1801 and won a second term in 1805. In these two terms he introduced many good policies, purchased from Napoleon, the French emperor (see page 15), the district in the south called Louisiana, for £3,000,000, and encouraged expansion west of the Mississippi river.

Jenner, Dr. Edward (1749–1823), English physician
Up to the end of the 18th century one of the most widespread –
and the most dangerous – diseases was smallpox. It struck regularly
and it was no respecter of class. Then, in 1796, a Gloucestershire
doctor, Edward Jenner, made an important discovery. Local
milkmaids who caught cowpox, a mild complaint and one common
to their trade, seemed to be completely unaffected when an epidemic
of smallpox struck the village. So Jenner thought that if he were to
inject a patient with a sample of cowpox serum, that patient ought
not to get smallpox. He tried it out on a small boy. First he gave him
cowpox serum. Then a few days later he injected smallpox serum.
Normally, this would have been fatal, but the boy was unharmed.

It was a major medical triumph. People could now be made
immune to the dread disease. Because the serum came from a cow,
Jenner called the process vaccination, from *vacca*, the Latin word
for cow.

Johnson, Dr. Samuel (1709–1784), English man of letters
For several years in the middle of the 18th century, one of the
best known men in London was Dr. Samuel Johnson. Ugly to look
at, with a loud voice, and an unparalleled wit, he was showered
with invitations to dinner parties, lunch and all sorts of other
gatherings. These qualities were but the external side of a profoundly
intelligent and extremely learned man, possibly the wisest man in
the country.

Johnson made his name in 1755 when he published his famous
Dictionary. This was a landmark in the history of the English
language. Thereafter, he mixed with the most celebrated people of
the day. His opinion was sought on all manner of things and his
advice was often taken – and found to be right.

Johnson was also a man of the greatest kindness and generosity.

Justinian I (AD 483–565), Byzantine emperor
The reign of the Byzantine emperor Justinian I (527–565) has been called the Golden Age of the Byzantine Empire. Certainly it was marked by three very important features, the recovery of much of the old Roman Empire in the west which had been lost to the barbarians, the re-writing of Roman law, and the building in Constantinople of St. Sophia's cathedral, perhaps the most magnificent church in the world.

Justinian was particularly interested in the law, and when he found the laws of the empire in a tangle, he appointed a committee of experts to re-frame them and, where necessary, reform them. Among the new clauses were some which paid special attention to women's rights which up to then had not counted for much. It is said that this was due to the influence of his wife, Theodora, a very domineering woman who for years seemed to be more powerful than even Justinian himself.

Justinian's Codes of Law are the basis of much of the law still used in Europe today.

Kelvin, Lord, William Thomson (1824–1907), Scottish physicist
William Thomson (later Lord Kelvin) was one of the most brilliant people ever to emerge in the British Isles. When only twenty-two he was appointed professor of natural philosophy at Glasgow University, one of the foremost scientific posts in the country. For fifty-three years he held the chair, and in that time he made a number of the most important discoveries of the century. He invented a range of mechanical and electrical contrivances, and he suggested a variety of scientific theories most of which have since been proved correct. These are just some of them: the absolute measurement of temperature (called the Kelvin scale), the mirror galvanometer, the tide predictor, the household electric meter, safety circuit fuses, dynamo electric machines.

Thomson became the world's leading expert on magnetism and he was the moving spirit in laying the first Atlantic cable, using

Brunel's great ship, the *Great Eastern*, to do it (see page 17). In some way or other he was involved with the majority of important developments of his century.

Thomson was knighted in 1866, and made a peer in 1892 when he took the title Lord Kelvin of Largs.

Knox, Dr. John (*c.* 1512–1572), Scottish religious reformer
John Knox is often thought to have hated women. But it was not so. It was only that he did not think they should be in positions of power in the state. This explains why he spent several years making fiery speeches against Mary, Queen of Scots. It did not help that while he was a devout Protestant, and had been the chief agent in converting Scotland to the new reformed faith, she was an equally devout Roman Catholic. As it happened, she did prove to be quite unfitted for power.

On one occasion, as a result of a particularly offensive speech against the queen, Mary had Knox arrested and brought for trial before the Privy Council for treason. But the Council acquitted him. This made him more popular than ever.

Scotland probably owes more to Knox than to any other man for its religious individuality.

Lavoisier, Antoine (1743–1794), French chemist
'Cut off his head! We have no need for men of science.' So spoke a member of the Revolutionary government in France in 1794 about Antoine Lavoisier to whom science owes an enormous debt.

This brilliant scientist, whose young days were covered with academic glory, held a number of posts as a government scientist. He was director of the state's gunpowder works in 1776, a member of the commission to establish a uniform system of weights and measures, from 1790. At the same time he carried out a number of original experiments in chemistry and physics. He showed that matter is indestructible. He proved that every chemical reaction could be expressed in terms of a chemical equation, and he devised the system of chemical naming which is still basically in use today.

The leaders of the French Revolution however, were suspicious of his power and he was arrested. His trial lasted only half a day and he was sent to the guillotine.

Lenin (1870–1924), Russian Communist leader
Lenin, whose real name was Vladimir Ilyitch Ulyanov, reconstructed the Russian state after the Revolution of 1917–18 which resulted in the murder of the Czar and his family, the exile of hundreds of noble and rich families, and the taking over by the state of all industry. What was the secret of Lenin's success?

This son of a civil servant was ruthless, harsh and intolerant of any ideas or opinions other than his own, but he was also an extremely determined leader who could get men to do anything he

wanted. He was involved in most of the revolutionary movements at the beginning of the century and on one occasion was banished to Siberia.

When the more moderate revolutionaries of 1917 had taken over the government, Lenin would not work with them but did everything he could to bring them down. The next year he succeeded in getting them voted out and in forming a new government with which he planned to build a new state.

What Lenin built was a worker's republic. This had to be done by the most brutal methods. Lenin believed that only force could bring about social change. Religion was crushed and the church deprived of any state support. Private property was seized and private trading was made unlawful. Farms were taken over and run on a collective basis. A secret police was formed to keep down all opposition. It was all effective and it was all terrifying. Millions of people died for their beliefs or because they simply did not fit into the new state.

At the height of this misery Lenin died.

Lincoln, Abraham (1809–1865), American president
Some Americans would say that Abraham Lincoln was the best of their presidents. Certainly his abolishing of slavery in America ranks as one of the great achievements of American history.

This tall, lean, rugged Kentucky-born lawyer was wise and tough, with an enormous amount of compassion for his fellow men. He was elected president in 1860 at a critical time in American history. The country was divided over the question of slavery. The northern states did not approve of it; the southern states claimed they had to have it to keep their sugar and cotton plantations going, and in 1861 the southern states broke away from the Union and formed a Confederacy of their own. Civil war followed.

Lincoln was determined to preserve the Union and also to abolish slavery. So he supported the northern states. At first the confederacy won some successes, but the superior strength of the north wore the confederates down and in 1865 they surrendered. Lincoln, meanwhile, had abolished slavery by a law of 1863.

Five days after the surrender, a mad actor called Booth fired a pistol at Lincoln in a theatre and in a few moments the great president died.

Lister, Joseph, 1st Lord (1827–1912), British surgeon
The two greatest problems in medicine have been the conquest of pain and the conquest of infection. The first victory in the former was won by W. T. G. Morton (see page 66). It was Joseph Lister, a British surgeon, who in the 1860s experimented with carbolic acid and introduced the practice of antisepsis, which dealt a major blow against infection.

The main danger to patients having operations was that their wounds became germ-infected, usually because of unhygienic conditions in the theatres and wards. In most cases death followed. So Lister tried to ensure that all surgery was done under hygienic conditions. He found that carbolic acid in solution was a reliable germ killer, and he devised a whole new routine for operations. Surgeons were to wash their hands and instruments were to be stored in carbolic acid. Nothing, not even a dressing, was to go near a patient without it having first been 'sterilised' with the solution. It was a remarkable advance, and thereafter the infection rate dropped sharply wherever the routine was employed. A whole new field of surgery now became possible as it was safe to do operations.

Livingstone, Dr. David (1813–1873), Scottish missionary
Livingstone was a doctor who, once qualified, decided to spend his life bringing relief to the sick among the African peoples. He was also a devout Christian with a burning desire to convert the Africans from their heathen beliefs into becoming Christians. These qualities made him an ideal person to send on missionary work and in 1840 the London Missionary Society asked him to go to Africa.

Livingstone also embarked on several journeys of exploration, for much of Africa was unknown then to Europeans. He discovered the Victoria Falls and Lake Nyasa. While searching for the source of the Nile he nearly died of exhaustion, and was only just rescued in time when the well-known journalist, Henry M. Stanley, who had gone out to Africa to look for him, found him.

Livingstone died in Africa, attended by his devoted African servants, but his body was brought home and buried in Westminster Abbey.

Longfellow, Henry Wadsworth (1807–1882), American poet
Longfellow is famous for creating the character of Hiawatha, in a long narrative poem called 'The Song of Hiawatha'. It tells the story of a Red Indian chief who had been sent among the Red Indians to teach them about peace. This American poet, who was professor of literature at Harvard university from 1836 to 1854, also wrote a great many other long poems, and some short ones as well. Some of these were as well known as Hiawatha, including 'The Wreck of the Hesperus', 'The Village Blacksmith' and 'Paul Revere's Ride'.

Longfellow is one of America's most famous poets, and many of his works have been set to music by American composers.

Luther, Martin (1483–1546), German religious reformer
In the 16th century many scholars and priests, having been able to read the New Testament in its original Greek form, found that the simple and direct ministry of Jesus Christ bore little resemblance to the elaborate trappings that surrounded the Roman Church. Agents were actually selling pieces of paper to humble peasants forgiving them their sins in return for money for the building of the new St. Peter's Cathedral in Rome, and there was nothing about this in the Bible.

Martin Luther, a German monk brought up in the strict Roman

tradition, was appalled at this and many other things he thought inconsistent, and in 1517 he decided to make a public protest. He drafted ninety-five objections and pinned them to the door of Wittenburg cathedral – and waited. The result was probably greater than he reckoned.

A fearful storm of argument followed, and for a while Luther was in some personal danger, but he had the protection of the king of Saxony. The row developed until nearly all Europe was involved in taking sides with Luther or the Roman Church. This came to be called the Reformation, for what Luther was urging was the reform of the Church and the re-statement of its doctrines in the light of what the New Testament taught.

Magellan, Ferdinand (1480–1521), Portuguese navigator

Magellan served the king of Portugal for a number of years as soldier and sailor, but in 1517 he quarrelled with him and went to Spain. There he put up a plan to the king to sail westwards across the Atlantic and find a route around America to the East Indies, as the Portuguese had the monopoly of the African sea route. The Spanish king liked the idea and financed a voyage.

In 1519 Magellan sailed, with five ships, down the eastern coast of South America, and after several months of terrible weather in which he lost two ships, he navigated through the difficult Straits to the Pacific Ocean. He knew roughly where the East Indies ought to be and he steered towards them, but he miscalculated the distance and the ships were afloat for three months, by the end of which the crews had run out of food and were eating sawdust and leather.

Finally, they landed in the Philippine Islands, then known as the Spice Islands. Magellan was killed a few days later in a skirmish with natives. One of his ships, however, came home across the Indian Ocean and round South Africa, thus making the first voyage round the whole world.

Marconi, Guglielmo (1874–1937), Italian scientist

When you turn a radio on, what you are doing is picking up signals sent out by various radio stations. The first man successfully to send and pick up signals over any distance was the Italian electrical scientist, Guglielmo Marconi who, before he came to work in Britain in 1895, had sent signals for distances up to a mile. Soon after his arrival in Britain he increased the distance for his signals up to about ten miles and by 1898 was exchanging messages with his operators in Europe.

In 1901, radio communication was established between Europe and America.

Marconi, who had an Irish mother and married into an Irish family, none the less kept his Italian nationality. The king of Italy made him a marchese (marquis) in 1929.

Marco Polo (1254–1324), Italian traveller

Marco Polo was the son of a Venetian merchant, Niccolo Polo who, with his brother Maffeo, set out in about 1260 to travel across Asia into the empire of the great Kublai Khan, grandson of Genghiz Khan (see page 45), whose capital was at Peking. They took young Marco with them and joined the caravan route through Tibet, along the famous Silk Route. When they reached Peking, they were welcomed by Kublai Khan who had ambitions to make better contact with the Western world.

The Polos returned to Venice in about 1270, with wonderful tales of what they had seen. Two years later, they set out again, taking Marco who was now eighteen. It was this voyage and its results that Marco was to write about. They went to China a different way this time, and it took four years to get to Peking. Kublai Khan again welcomed them and gave Marco a job in government service. Marco served in one capacity or another including a governor of a province, for nearly seventeen years.

The Polos once more decided to go home, in about 1290, taking with them precious stones and all manner of wonderful Chinese things. Marco's book was a great success in Europe. It led to an upsurge in trading between China and the Western World.

Marlborough, John Churchill, 1st Duke of (1650–1722), English soldier and statesman

Britain has produced many great generals, but it is acknowledged that the greatest of all was Marlborough. When well over fifty, and never having commanded a large army before, he led a combined force of British, Dutch, German and Austrian troops against the French and Spanish at Blenheim in Bavaria in 1704 and utterly defeated them. Three more victories against France, at Ramillies in 1706, at Oudenarde in 1708, and at Malplaquet in 1709, completed the most remarkable campaign and led directly to France, then the most powerful nation in Europe, seeking peace.

A grateful nation built for Marlborough and his wife a splendid home near Woodstock in Oxfordshire, which was called Blenheim Palace.

John Churchill entered the army quite young and served with members of the royal family. By the time of James II's reign (1685–1688) he had become influential in state affairs. He was one of the politicians who invited the Dutch prince, William of Orange, to England to become William III in place of James who had to abdicate for ruling so badly. Churchill served William well at first, but then plotted with the exiled James to restore him to his throne. William put him in the Tower of London but soon released him, though he never trusted him again.

Before William died in 1702 he had appointed Churchill, now Earl of Marlborough, as Commander-in-Chief of the Allied Forces against Louis XIV of France. His successor Queen Anne, who had long favoured him, made him a Duke and gave him the scope for displaying his wonderful military gifts.

Marx, Karl (1818–1883), German founder of Communism
Karl Marx is regarded as the founder of Communism, though it is likely that if he were alive today he would not approve of the way this system of living is being pursued in Russia and Eastern European countries.

Marx, a German Jewish scholar, studied closely the revolutionary ideas which were growing up in Europe in the 1840s, and in 1848, with Friedrich Engels, another scholar, he produced the Communist Manifesto. This book pointed the way to workers seizing control of factories and eventually running the state.

Marx came to England in 1849 and stayed here for the rest of his life. Most of the time he studied at the British Museum or addressed meetings of early socialist movements. His greatest work, probably, was *Das Kapital*, but it did not earn him much money, and he had to depend largely on his friend, Engels, who had set up a business in Manchester which was a success.

Michelangelo (1475–1564), Italian artistic genius
Michelangelo was almost as important in the artistic achievements of the Italian Renaissance as Leonardo da Vinci (see page 36). A sculptor, painter and architect, his first major work was a huge statue of David, king of the Hebrews, hewn out of marble. It made him famous all over Italy, and thenceforth the demand for his services was always much greater than even his genius and immense capacity for work could provide. And yet this man who wrote some of the loveliest verse in the Italian language, was unhappy, and continually complained of shortage of money, even though he was generally highly paid.

Among his great works was the painting of the ceiling of the Sistine Chapel in the Vatican, which took four years. He painted most of it lying on his back on some scaffolding. Soon after finishing this he was given the chance to design the chapel of St. Lorenzo in Florence, and here he also sculpted the statues.

Michelangelo was deeply shocked when Rome was sacked by troops of Charles V in 1527 and his work thereafter reflects his great disappointment in Mankind. All the same, the quality, the vigour and the grandeur of his work continued unabated. He was appointed architect to the new St. Peter's Cathedral in Rome, and he designed many of its main features, in particular the marvellous dome.

It is said that in his last days he was regarded as a superhuman genius, and men called him 'The Divine'.

Molière (1622–1673), French actor-manager and playwright
The French have produced many great playwrights, and the greatest writer of comedies was Molière, the stage name of Jean Baptiste Poquelin.

Molière studied the plays of Greek and Latin authors while he was at college and he probably acted in some of them, too. When he was twenty-one he inherited some money and with it formed a theatrical company to produce plays in Paris. He had no luck there: the competition was too great and he lost nearly all his money. So he tried in the provinces, where over about thirteen years he produced and acted in many comedies. These were much more successful.

This led him to return to Paris and try again, and this time Louis XIV heard of him, became interested, and offered some support.

During these years Molière wrote a number of very funny plays, usually poking fun at pompous or shallow people. He mocked at hypocrisy and superstition and many other vices that seemed to affect educated people of the day. His best known plays were *Le Misanthrope*, *Tartuffe*, and *Le Malade Imaginaire*.

More, Sir Thomas (1478–1535), English scholar and statesman
Thomas More was just one of the many able men that Henry VIII used and then discarded because they did not do what they were told.

This brilliant, kind, saintly scholar and lawyer, who wrote a book called *Utopia*, which was a land where everybody shared everything and people could believe what they wanted, was appointed Lord Chancellor in 1529. Henry VIII believed he could get More to support him in all his policies, especially the religious ones. At first the two men worked well together, for More believed that the Church required some reform, but when the king determined to break forever with the Church of Rome and make himself Supreme Head of the English Church, More would not go along with him. The ungrateful king had him charged with high treason (it was treason, said the king, to disobey him). Of course, More was found guilty, and he was executed.

Morse, Samuel (1791–1872), American inventor
Samuel Morse began life as a painter, and even became president of the National Academy of Design in the United States of America. Then in about 1832, he became interested in telegraphy, and over the next ten or so years he worked on a telegraphic code which came to bear his name, the Morse Code. This system of signals for communicating alphabetic letters, numbers, and punctuation marks was

based on elements which were long (dashes), or short (dots), the former being three times longer than the latter. These could be represented by buzzing, lamp flashes, flag movements or zig-zag lines on paper.

It was a very important innovation in communication, but Morse was involved in long battles in American law courts to prove he had invented the code. In the end he won, and in his last years he became a very rich man.

Morton, W. T. G. (1819–1868), American discoverer of anaesthetics. It may seem hard to believe that less than 150 years ago people had to have operations without any kind of anaesthetic. But this was all changed in 1846, at the Massachusetts General Hospital in Boston, U.S.A., when a young American dentist, William Thomas Green Morton, gave a patient a whiff of ether – and put him to sleep. Immediately, the surgeon, the famous Dr. Warren, lifted a scalpel from the instrument tray and began to make swift strokes through the patient's neck, and within minutes he had removed a growth which had been causing a lot of pain.

A few moments later, the patient awoke, and said he had felt nothing.

It was a sensational moment in medical history. Before long the development of anaesthetics was of the utmost importance to doctors and surgeons everywhere, and nowadays an anaesthetic is automatically given before surgery.

Morton, a great benefactor to humanity, received little credit for his discovery. Jealous scientists tried to belittle his achievement and some even said he had stolen the idea from someone else. It is tragic to relate that he died in great poverty and misery.

Mozart, Wolfgang Amadeus (1756–1791), Austrian composer
In his short life, Mozart composed a vast amount of music of all kinds, orchestral, operatic, and instrumental, It is generally agreed that most

of it ranks among the very best music ever written.

Mozart was striking chords on a harpsichord at the age of three, and composing short pieces a year or two later. At six he was performing in public and by 1769, when he was only thirteen, he was concert-master at Salzburg. By now he had begun to compose longer and greater works. He was also making a name for improvisation, that is, making up melodies and pieces on the spot.

To list his works would take pages. A German scholar, Kochel, spent years cataloguing them, and today his numbering is used to distinguish the compositions, for example, the Linz symphony in C major, K, 425. Among Mozart's best loved works are the operas *Don Giovanni*, *Cosi Fan Tutti*, and *The Magic Flute*, the symphonies Number 40 and Number 41, and the Number 24 piano concerto in C minor.

His seemingly inexhaustible energy and limitless flow of musical ideas, together with his extravagant way of living and the resulting frequent shortages of money, brought him to a very early death aged only thirty-five.

Mussolini, Benito (1883–1945), Italian dictator
Mussolini was the son of an Italian blacksmith. At the end of the First World War, when the Italian state was in danger of being broken up by Communists, he formed a party, called the Fascist Party, and organised a march on Rome demanding a new government to include himself and some fascist colleagues. The king, Victor Emanuel III, dreading civil war, invited him to form a government.

From 1922 to 1943, Mussolini ruled Italy as a dictator. Though he achieved some good things like reviving the economy, building many miles of straight roads (called autostrada) and providing full employment, his rule was also harsh, cruel and terrifying. Like Hitler in Germany (see page 50) he crushed all opposition by means of secret police, prison camps and torture.

In 1935, in an attempt to build a new Roman empire he invaded Abyssinia, in north-east Africa. In 1940 he entered the Second

World War on Hitler's side. His armies, however, were not of the stuff of ancient Rome: they were badly led, poorly equipped and the men lacked the courage needed for war. He invaded Greece in 1941 and was only saved from disaster by help from Hitler which seriously affected Hitler's own plans to invade Russia. In North Africa his armies were scattered by the British. By 1943 the Allies were invading Italy itself.

Mussolini was finally dismissed by the king in July 1943 and the Italians surrendered. He was rescued by the Germans and restored to his dictatorship, but it was an empty position. At the end of the war he was seized by patriots who hanged him, exhibiting his body upside down in Milan.

Nelson, Vice-Admiral 1st Viscount (1758–1805), English admiral. No one would question that Nelson was one of the greatest admirals in world history. He was incredibly brave; his naval strategy was brilliant in plan and extremely successful in being carried out; he was never defeated; and he was adored by all ranks in the navy. What is more, by his destruction of the French and Spanish fleets at Trafalgar in 1805, which cost him his life, he wrecked Napoleon's plans for invading Britain and ruined his chances of controlling the seas, which was vital for him if he wanted to dominate Europe.

Horatio Nelson was born in Norfolk. He went to sea when very young. Although he was sickly, pale and of very small height, he made up for this – and more – in courage. In one of his first actions he lost an eye, and in another he lost his right arm. By the time he was thirty-eight he was second in command at the battle of St. Vincent where it was really his skill that won the day.

In 1798 he won the first of his three great victories, at Aboukir Bay in Egypt, on the Nile. This prevented Napoleon (see page 15) from leading his French armies across Asia into British India. Three years later he destroyed the Danish fleet off Copenhagen and knocked the Danes out of the war. Here, he disobeyed the orders of the commander-in-chief, Sir Hyde Parker, who had ordered him to retire, by holding a telescope to his blind eye and exclaiming to his colleagues: 'I really do not see the signal.' Thereupon he bore down upon the enemy and scattered their ships.

Despite these splendid victories which were among the boldest and most skilful in all naval history, the Admiralty, staffed with people who were jealous of his success and his popularity, did not employ him for many months. But in 1803 he was made commander of the British fleet in the Mediterranean and he set out to try to smash the French fleet.

At Cape Trafalgar in October 1805 he broke up the combined French and Spanish fleets, sinking fourteen ships and crippling many more. In the heat of the action, however, a French sniper in the rigging of one of their ships, shot Nelson through the spine and the gallant admiral died an hour or so later down in the sick bay. Before he died, however, he heard of the magnitude of the victory, and his last thoughts were for his country. 'Thank God,' he said, 'I have done my duty.'

Newton, Sir Isaac (1642–1727), English physicist and mathematician

Newton once noticed that when apples fell off a tree they descended at a speed that varied according to the distance they had to travel to the ground. He deduced from this that the earth itself has a pulling force, and this led him to pronounce the laws of gravitation. He then used these laws to explain the motions of the earth, the moon and the planets in the Solar System, and in furthering this he constructed a reflecting telescope with which to study the heavens more closely. This in turn led him to discover the composition of light.

These are but a few of the ideas and achievements of this astonishingly brilliant scientist who was professor of mathematics at Cambridge for thirty-two years (1669–1701). Others included the differential calculus, and the famous Laws of Motion which are the basis of modern mechanics.

In his own time Newton was greatly admired and respected not only for his brilliance but also for the modesty with which he demonstrated it.

Nobel, Alfred (1833–1896), Swedish inventor
Alfred Nobel was a Swedish engineer who in 1866 invented dynamite – by accident. He was making some nitroglycerine, a highly explosive liquid which blows up at the slightest provocation, when a flask of it slipped out of his hands and fell – into a box of fine powder. Miraculously, the liquid did not explode; instead it was absorbed by the powder. Nobel noticed that the mixture formed a sort of paste which could be shaped and packed into a container. He experimented by detonating the container outside in a field and it exploded. He had found a safe way to handle nitroglycerine.

Nobel realised the potential value in warfare of this mixture, which he called dynamite, from the Greek word meaning power.

He saw that if it was used skilfully it could kill hundreds of people at one go. He also hoped that once nations used it they would appreciate its terrible power and might therefore think about abandoning war as an answer to disagreements.

His discovery brought him a lot of money but it did not stop wars. So, when he died he left his fortune for five prizes to be awarded every year to eminent scientists, authors and workers for peace.

Pasteur, Louis (1822–1895), French chemist
Pasteur discovered the existence of germs. He found that they could be killed by applying heat, and from this came his process of pasteurisation. He also discovered an inoculation against the dangerous disease of anthrax, and he found a cure for hydrophobia, or rabies, a dread disease which arose from the bite of a mad dog. His work on germs led England's Lord Lister (see page 58) to develop the antiseptic system.

This brilliant French chemist achieved so much that in the last days of his life he was honoured everywhere. There was one special ceremony in Paris in 1892, held to celebrate his seventieth birthday, when Lister came forward in front of a huge crowd of the greatest men of science and offered the homage of the medical and scientific world to him. With tears in his eyes, Pasteur clasped Lister in his arms and begged him to share in the praise. And the great men all stood up and cheered.

Pericles (*c.* 490–429 BC), Greek (Athenian) statesman
If you ever go to Athens you will see on a hill the vast and splendid structure called the Parthenon. This great temple is a constant reminder of the man who had it built, Pericles, perhaps the greatest ruler ancient Greece ever had.

Pericles was elected to the board of commoners, a sort of council which governed the Athenian state, in 461 BC. He proved so popular that he was elected time and again and thus became virtual ruler of the state. It was said that he was incorruptible, that is, he would not take bribes, and that even those who opposed him also admired him. He believed that men were good at heart and only needed guidance to keep on the right path. This belief dominated his policies as head of the government.

The Greeks had not long been experimenting with democratic government, that is, rule by a number of representatives elected to govern by the votes of all free people. Pericles made this democracy work better. Representatives had their backgrounds examined to see if they were qualified to serve. Anyone who had any dealings with public money was carefully supervised so that corruption and theft were made more difficult. In his time people really felt they were taking part in government.

To the great grief of all Athenians this splendid ruler died in a fearful plague which struck Athens in 429 BC.

Pizarro, Francisco (c. 1470–1541), Spanish conqueror of Peru
There had been great civilisations in Peru since at least 1500 BC. The last and greatest was the Inca civilisation, which dominated that part of South America from about AD 1100 to 1530. In that year Pizarro, a Spanish adventurer, who had tried unsuccessfully to make a living in Panama, led an expedition by sea and landed on the Peruvian coast. Then he marched inland and attacked the capital city of Atahualpa, the reigning emperor, or Inca, as he was called.

Although Pizarro, like Cortez in Mexico (see page 32) had a small force, he had guns and horses which the Peruvians had never seen. By a trick, Pizarro captured Atahualpa and then began to steal all the gold and silver that he and his men could find. Atahualpa was promised his freedom if he would fill up a room with gold and silver, but when he had done this he was treacherously put to death. The Inca government collapsed because its leader, who made all the decisions, had gone.

Pizarro and his men behaved appallingly. In 1541 Pizarro was murdered, but this did not change the fact that the Spaniards had destroyed a wonderful civilisation.

Pythagoras (*c.* 530 BC), Greek mathematician
Pythagoras was a brilliant Greek mathematician and thinker who settled in the Greek colony of Croton in Italy in about 530 BC. There he set up a kind of college where people could meditate about abstract subjects such as what happens to the soul when the body dies.

He himself was very interested in geometry, astronomy and physics. He proposed the theorem that bears his name, that the square on the hypotenuse of a right angled triangle equals the sum of the squares on the other two sides. He is said to have suggested that the earth moved round the sun, some 2000 years before Copernicus (see page 31). He also showed that tightening or loosening a piece of wire held between two clamps varies the musical note obtained by plucking the wire, and that by doing this at regular intervals a harmonic scale is produced.

Rachmaninov, Sergei (1873–1943), Russian composer and pianist.
It is difficult to say whether this great Russian musician was better at composing music or playing the piano. Today, listening to such well-loved works as the 'Second Piano Concerto in C Minor', or the 'Rhapsody on a theme of Paganini', one would put him high in the list of romantic composers to whom melody was as important as structure. But if you heard him play it was something you never forgot. He could make a piano sing as no one had since Liszt who was probably the greatest pianist of all time.

Rachmaninov composed most of his work in his earlier years in Russia. At the time of the Revolution in 1917 he left, and after about twenty years touring the world playing at concerts and enriching the musical experiences of millions of people, he settled in the United States.

Richelieu, Cardinal le Duc de (1585–1642), French statesman

It has been said that the history of France between the death of Henry IV in 1610 and the year 1642 is much the same thing as the story of one man, Armand Jean du Plessis de Richelieu. Certainly this astonishing man played a decisive part in French affairs at home and abroad in those years.

Although a priest, and later a cardinal, Richelieu was also adviser first to the widow of Henry IV and then to her son, Louis XIII when he came of age. He had one aim – to make France the greatest power in Europe – and through his will-power and his unchallengeable political gifts he achieved it.

At home he crushed the power of the nobles by blowing up their castles and prohibiting private armies. He introduced a new system of government through superintendents of regions who had wide local powers but who were directly dependent upon and responsible to him. Abroad he supported the Protestant countries in the Thirty Years' War, even though he was a Catholic, because he wanted to break the power of the Catholic league of states. He supported the Portuguese in their struggle against Spain as he considered Spain too dangerous for European peace. He also encouraged French navigators and traders to found the French empire in the New World and in the East.

Richelieu died in 1642 and was followed by his first assistant, Mazarin.

Robespierre, Maximilien (1758–1794), French revolutionary leader. When one thinks of Robespierre one cannot help thinking also of the screaming noise of the blade of the guillotine as it slithers down the grooves on to someone's neck to cut his head off. For Robespierre, the most extreme leader of the French revolutionaries, sent hundreds of people, many of them innocent, to their deaths on this hideous machine. And yet at heart he was the mildest and most good mannered of men, and quite incorruptible.

In 1789 he was a lawyer and a delegate to the National Assembly when the Revolution broke out. As time went by he felt that the first leaders were not uprooting enough of the hatred traditions and institutions of the old regime, and he managed, by a mixture of oratory, behind-the-scenes management and driving power, to get rid of the moderates like Danton and Hebert who had been his friends. Then he took over control in 1793 and began a reign of terror which lasted a year. In that time he sent almost anyone who opposed him to the guillotine. But by the middle of 1794 he had gone too far, and some moderates arrested him and put him to death – on the guillotine.

Roosevelt, Franklin D. (1882–1945), American president
Franklin Roosevelt is the only American to be elected president four times, and in his case it was four times in succession. It was a remarkable achievement, more so when you know that he spent the best part of his working life in a wheel chair following a crippling attack of infantile paralysis.

A lawyer and politician, Roosevelt was a cousin of Theodore Roosevelt (see page 76) and he won his first election in 1932. This was in the period of the Great Depression, when American business had been through a big slump. Roosevelt offered the nation a New Deal, as he called it, sweeping reforms which would make America strong and rich again, with more jobs. To the greatest measure he succeeded, and in 1936 he was overwhelmingly re-elected president, and again in 1940.

In 1941 he brought the United States into the Second World War on Britain's side and his country was partly responsible for the defeat of both Germany and Japan. He was re-elected president for a fourth time in 1944 but towards the end of that year his health began to fail and he made some bad judgements. Suddenly, a few weeks before the end of the war in Europe was over, he died of a heart attack.

Roosevelt, Theodore (1858–1919), American president

Although the United States made huge strides in becoming a powerful and highly industrialised nation in the 19th century, it was not until this century that she began to play any major part in world affairs. And the man who put America on the world map, as it were, was Theodore Roosevelt. This cheerful, boisterous and very able soldier-turned-politician had been an excellent governor of New York. Then in 1900 he was made vice-president of the United States and when President McKinley was assassinated the following year Roosevelt succeeded him.

Roosevelt awakened the American people to the fact that they were a great people, capable of playing an international role. In 1905 he managed to get Russia and Japan to stop their war of 1904–5, and in 1908 he sent the American fleet on a world tour to show how impressive it was. He made American influence felt in all directions, and it has remained dominant ever since.

Rutherford, Professor Lord (1871–1937), New Zealand born physicist

Up to 1919 only a few scientists realised that the atom was not the smallest particle of matter. Even then they did not know how to break one up. Then, in that year, Sir Ernest Rutherford, professor of physics at Manchester University, bombarded the nucleus of a nitrogen atom with radioactive particles from radium, and he converted the nucleus into a number of nuclei of hydrogen. In fact, he had split the atom.

It was a sensational achievement, and it opened up a whole new field of science, nuclear physics, which was to lead to the invention of the nuclear bomb, but also to the development of the generation of electricity by nuclear power.

This stocky, booming-voiced New Zealander, whose whole academic life was but a catalogue of research successes, dominated the scientific world for a generation and played the leading part in all nuclear research. He collected all the top prizes awarded to distinguished scientists. He also gathered round him, when he was professor of physics at Cambridge from 1919 to 1937, the most brilliant collection of young physicists and gave them the kind of example and encouragement that no man has done before or since. At the height of his powers he died suddenly, when he was sixty-six.

Shakespeare, William (1564–1616), English poet and playwright. The output of the English poet and playwright Shakespeare was enormous, and it is generally regarded as the highest expression of English literary genius. Plays like *Macbeth, Julius Caesar, Hamlet, The Merchant of Venice, A Midsummer Night's Dream,* are performed more often than any written by anyone else. And there is no doubt at all about their quality, the beautiful language, the humour, the characterisation and the drama.

Yet about the author we know almost nothing. Indeed, men have doubted ever since he died whether Shakespeare ever wrote a line.

William Shakespeare, a Stratford-upon-Avon resident, was first heard of as an actor in London at the age of thirty. Thereafter a stream of plays and poems appeared over the next twenty or so years under his name. He seems to have earned a good living for he bought one of the largest houses in Stratford. Finally, he retired in 1610 and died six years later.

Shaw, George Bernard (1856–1950), Irish playwright and wit Bernard Shaw lived for nearly a century. For the second half of his life he was one of the most famous men in the world. Whether it was in a play or a book or a newspaper article or a recorded interview, he was always saying startling things. Sometimes they were outrageous. He said that Lord Lister (see page 58), the greatest surgeon in British history, was a half-wit and a menace. Sometimes they were wise, especially when he told the Western World to stop worrying about Russian aims: one had only to look at a map to see that the Russians had more problems than anybody else.

Shaw's commentaries covered every aspect of life. If he did not always speak from deep knowledge, he did speak from observation. He never drank, he did not eat meat, he did not smoke, and he hated cruelty of any kind. His words, whether in print or on radio or on film, were punctuated with wit and humour, behind which lay a good deal of common sense.

Shaw wrote many plays. Each one had a lengthy preface to it, which argued the points he was trying to make in the play's dialogue. Among the best known were *Pygmalion*, *Man and Superman*, *The Doctor's Dilemma* (an attack on orthodox medicine) and *Saint Joan*, perhaps the most dramatic of them all. He often said of himself that he was better than Shakespeare. That may seem boastful now, but who can say whether in 100 years time other people will not be saying it as well?

Socrates (*c.* 470–*c.* 400 BC), Greek thinker
Socrates is probably best known as the Greek thinker and teacher who was forced to drink hemlock and die for, as the accusation went, corrupting youth. Of course, he did nothing of the kind; he merely taught young people how to think for themselves, to question authority in some cases, but not to disobey it.

He left no works himself but his most celebrated pupil, Plato, wrote accounts of their long and very absorbing conversations, and of his trial, too, and this is how we know what kind of man he was. He was always searching for truth, always anxious to make the complex problems of life clearer and more easily understood. This meant questioning many religious and political beliefs, and this is how he aroused the anger of influential men who succeeded in getting him sentenced to death.

Solomon (*c.* 990–*c.* 930 BC), king of the Hebrews
Solomon was the son of king David whose career is written about in the two books of Samuel in the Old Testament. In about 970 BC,

young Solomon became king, and he devoted his life to making the Hebrew state strong, improving the buildings in Jerusalem and reforming the tax system. As he was not a military leader like his warrior father, he concentrated on keeping at peace with his neighbours by advantageous treaties of alliance with them, especially with the Phoenicians who dominated the East Mediterranean.

The biggest building project of Solomon's reign was a new temple to the Hebrew God at Jerusalem. It took fourteen years to complete and it was decorated with the finest ornament obtainable anywhere. The temple came to mean a great deal to the Hebrews – and to their descendants the Jews.

Soon after his death the Hebrew state divided into two, Israel and Judah.

Stalin, Joseph (1879–1953), Russian dictator
Joseph Stalin, whose real name was Joseph Vissarionovitch Dzhugashvili, was born in Georgia. In 1898, while studying theology, he joined a socialist organisation and came under the influence of Marxism. He became involved in revolutionary propaganda and agitation and joined the Social Democrat party early in its history.

When Lenin (see page 56) became master of the new Soviet Union, in 1918, Stalin had a major post in the government.

Lenin died in 1924 and at once a power struggle followed between Stalin and another of Lenin's associates, Trotsky, undoubtedly a more able man. Stalin, however, managed to get Trotsky expelled and he then ruled Russia as a dictator for the next twenty-seven years. In 1936 he staged great 'Purge' trials to exterminate anyone who might have been able to overthrow him and form an alternate government.

During the Second World War he took control of the Soviet armed forces when the Nazis invaded Russia in 1941 and he was largely responsible, through his inspiration, for the ultimate success of Russian arms against the Germans. After the war he dominated the various peace talks and succeeded in getting many Eastern European countries to choose Communist governments, which would do more or less what he wanted. He died in 1953 still absolute master of his people.

Stephenson, George (1781–1848), English railway engineer

George Stephenson was brought up in very humble circumstances near Newcastle-upon-Tyne. His father worked in a coal mine, and almost as soon as he was old enough George joined him. In the evenings, however, he was determined to educate himself and for years he studied many subjects, including mechanical engineering.

One of the things he noticed about the working of the coal mine was the enormous amount of effort needed to drag coal-filled tubs along the iron track from the pit head to the storage bay, whether they were pulled by men or by horses. So, with his new-found knowledge he built a steam locomotive to do the job. Before long this successful idea led him to think up railway carriages for human beings, pulled by locomotives, and in 1825 he built an engine which pulled carriages along the first passenger line, from Stockton to Darlington.

Five years later he built his famous locomotive, the Rocket, which ran from Liverpool to Manchester. The railway age had begun.

Sun Yat-Sen (1866–1925), Chinese republican leader

Sun Yat-Sen became a doctor because he wanted to help fight the many diseases which were widespread in China in the late 19th century. Much of this misery was due to the lack of concern of the Chinese emperors, the Manchus as they were called, and when people began to plot revolution Sun Yat-Sen joined them, and soon began to organise attacks on the government. His activities got him into trouble and he had to live abroad for some years.

Then in 1911 he returned during a serious revolt which ousted the Manchus, and he was proclaimed President of the Republic of

China. At once there was more trouble. Half of China did not want him, so he stepped down. Anarchy followed for some years.

It distressed Sun Yat-Sen that he was unable to do anything for China. The country did not want to unite. Towards the end of his life there seemed to be a chance of unity under Chiang Kai-Shek, but that was shattered when the Japanese invaded China in 1931.

Swift, Jonathan (1667–1745), Irish writer
Gulliver's Travels is one of the most amusing books in the English language, and although it was really meant as a satire on British politics as they were in the early 18th century, the book has been enjoyed as much by children as by adults ever since.

It was written by the leading political commentator of the day, Jonathan Swift, an Irish-born clergyman and scholar who spent many years travelling between Ireland where he had a parish and London where he discussed all manner of things with the greatest men in politics, religion, law and literature. His biting criticisms of prominent statesmen, sometimes in language that would not be permitted today, went a long way towards discrediting them – which it was meant to do. He was particularly biting towards the Duke of Marlborough (see page 62) who was accused of misusing national funds while he was in command in Europe.

The last years of Swift's life were unhappy, as his mind began to break down.

Tasman, Abel (1603–1659), Dutch explorer
In 1642 Tasman was appointed to command an expedition to chart the western coast of Australia. He was sent out by van Dieman, the governor-general of the Dutch East Indies, based in Java.

Tasman sailed right round the western and southern coasts and landed on the island of Tasmania, which he called van Dieman's Land. Then he went on and found the west coast of the southern island of New Zealand. Here, the Maoris attacked him so he set off again and returned to Java. In 1644 he sailed again to Australia, discovered the Gulf of Carpentaria and charted the north coast.

Unfortunately neither he nor the Dutch appreciated what he had achieved, and it was many years before Australia and New Zealand were opened up to Europeans.

Tchaikovski, Peter Ilyitch (1840–1893), Russian composer

Tchaikovski was a law student in St. Petersburg (now called Leningrad) and was also an accomplished pianist. When he qualified and got a job in the Ministry of Justice, he found his work very unsatisfying. Music increasingly dominated his life and he felt a burning desire to compose. So he gave up the job and went to the St. Petersburg Conservatoire, one of the best music schools in Europe.

Tchaikovski now began to compose and his music differed greatly from that of his contemporaries. It was essentially Russian; it was highly emotional; and it was filled with contrast. He composed several symphonies and piano concertos, the first one of the latter being by far the most widely enjoyed. As he was a very unhappy person – he had made a bad marriage in 1877, and missed his mother greatly – much of his music reveals his misery. Apart from symphonies and concertos, he also wrote ballet music, and indeed may be said to have lifted this new art form to a very high level by the exquisite nature of his music. 'The Swan Lake' is his best known ballet suite.

Themistocles (c. 520–c. 460 BC), Greek statesman

This remarkable Greek politician came to prominence in Athens shortly after the battle of Marathon in 490 BC. He warned the Greeks that though Darius I (see page 34) of Persia had lost there, the Persians would try to conquer Greece again. So he persuaded them to build up their navy, and when in 480 BC, Darius' son, Xerxes, invaded Greece, Themistocles was appointed to command the fleet. By his initiative and skill the Greeks destroyed Xerxes' fleet at a great battle off Salamis. Then Themistocles persuaded the Spartans to attack the Persians the following year, at Plataea, and this they did, winning a great victory.

The Greeks ought to have been grateful to Themistocles, but the Spartans resented him and eventually persuaded the Athenians to bring charges against him of having misused public money. The charges were almost certainly false, but Themistocles was banished. After many adventures he came to Persia where he was given asylum.

Timurlaine (1336–1405), Mongol conqueror
Timurlaine was a descendant of Genghiz Khan (see page 45) and was born in central Asia. When he grew up he was very much like Genghiz, but with more personal charm. He decided to rebuild his ancestor's great empire which had, because of its size, proved too big to be managed except by a man of the highest qualities. So Timurlaine trained and equipped a large, highly mobile army of cavalrymen and foot soldiers and then set out on a path of conquest.

One after the other the states fell, Persia, Afghanistan, India (where he captured Delhi in 1398), Asia Minor and Turkey. Then he set out on the biggest expedition of his career, the invasion of China. But at the moment of departure, in 1405, he was taken ill and died almost at once. His empire broke up as he left no one capable of holding it together or managing it.

Trajan (AD 53–117), Roman emperor
The Roman Empire reached its widest extent through the great military achievements of Marcus Ulpius Traianus (Trajan), a distinguished Roman field commander who became emperor in AD 98.

Trajan had attracted the attention of the emperor Nerva who, not having a son of his own, adopted him as heir, confident that the young general would prove a good and successful ruler. His belief could not have been better justified.

Trajan ensured the safety of the empire by crushing enemies along its border, including the Dacians, the Parthians and the Germans. At home he determined through wise government to establish prosperity in the empire. The power of the Senate, increasingly sapped by a run of dictatorial emperors, was restored in large measure. And the empire's finances were properly run, the example being set at the imperial court itself where considerable cuts in spending were introduced.

When Trajan died he left the empire peaceful, contented and rich.

Trevithick, Richard (1771–1833), British engineer
Richard Trevithick was an engineer in a Cornish mine. In his spare time he interested himself in steam engineering, and at the turn of the 19th century he devised a number of new machines. These included a high pressure steam engine in 1801 with which he propelled a road carriage, the first ever to be driven in England.

Trevithick applied a steam engine to a locomotive to pull trucks along railway lines, and also to machinery and for rock-boring and dredging.

In 1816 he went to South America to put his talents at the disposal of the revolutionaries who were fighting for independence from Spain. When he came back eleven years later, he found he had been completely forgotten in England. As he had lost all his money in South America, he died in great poverty.

Vespucci, Amerigo (1451–1512), Italian born explorer
Amerigo Vespucci was an Italian sailor who joined several expeditions to the New World after Columbus' epic voyage to the West Indies. In 1500 as a member of the Ojeda expedition which actually reached the mainland of South America, he claimed to be the discoverer of the continent. The claim was hotly contested.

In 1507, Vespucci explored the Gulf of Mexico, and a German

geographer, Waldseemuller, suggested that the land there should be named after Amerigo, and in this way both continents came to be known as America. It was one of those inexplicable situations of history, for there were many other navigators after whom the New World could have been named, most notably Columbus who had landed on the mainland more than once.

Walpole, Sir Robert (1676–1745), English statesman
Walpole was not only the first Prime Minister of Great Britain. He also held the office for longer, without a break, than anyone else has done (1721–1742).

This jovial, easy-going and efficient man rendered the greatest service to his country. He was appointed head of the government by George I in 1721. It was a reward for having pulled the nation round after the scandal of the South Sea Bubble, a series of financial ventures in which thousands of people had invested – and lost – most of their money. Members of the government had been involved and had made money, and Walpole had, without fear or favour, compelled them and others to pay it back.

Walpole now set about rebuilding the economy of the nation. In twenty-one years he kept the country out of major wars and enabled it to benefit from the new machines which were bringing industrialisation, and from revolutionary farming methods. By 1742, when he was dismissed because he did not want to take part in a war in Europe, Britain was the most advanced nation in the world, a position held until the end of the 19th century.

Washington, George (1732–1799), first American president
It is doubtful if any American has been held in such esteem as George Washington. It was not so much his dash and brilliance as commander of the colonists' armies in the War of Independence (1774–1783), nor yet his tenure of office as first president of the new republic of the United States (1789–1793 and 1793–1797). Rather it

was the great honesty and integrity of his character. It was said that 'George Washington never told a lie'. Whether this was true or not, it was believed by most Americans and so they accorded him a respect bordering on reverence.

Washington served as an officer in the British controlled army in the American colonies, but when the help given by the colonists to Britain in her war with France over Canada was rewarded not with gratitude but with extra taxes and no representation in parliament, the colonists rebelled. Washington joined them and after war broke out he was appointed commander of their army, as he was the most experienced officer they had.

The colonists won, due largely to Washington's organisation and his fine, bold leadership. When the United States Republic was created, and its Constitution formed in 1787, he played a leading part, and not surprisingly he was elected first president. He was persuaded to stand again in 1793, but refused to be elected for a third time.

Watt, James (1736–1819), Scottish engineer

James Watt is often credited with having invented the steam engine. Actually, it was invented by Newcomen, though his machine was not effective as a power unit. Watt developed a separate condenser for the steam, applied it to a Newcomen engine, and so made the steam engine a practical idea. He can therefore be said to have been the first person to make a steam engine produce usable power.

This cheerful and brilliant Scottish engineer and inventor had had a remarkable boyhood. It is said that at six he could solve almost any geometrical problem, and that at fourteen he knew enough about steam engineering to work out how he would improve Newcomen's model.

Watt went into business as a manufacturer with Matthew Boulton, and in his time he also invented the marine screw propeller, and the centrifugal governor for regulating engine speeds.

Wellington, Arthur Wellesley, 1st Duke of (1769–1852), British soldier and statesman

When the Duke of Wellington was an old man, people all over the country used to write to him or consult him about almost everything. They might ask him to recommend an invention: they might ask him his views on some obscure religious argument. Even the queen, Victoria, and her husband, Prince Albert, scarcely ever made any major decisions without first getting his advice. Such was the veneration held by the nation for this remarkable man. How had he earned it?

Arthur Wellesley, born in Ireland of an Anglo-Irish noble family, entered the army. His first big command was in India, against a rebel chief, Tippoo Sahib, and in the campaign against Tippoo Wellesley covered himself with glory by his bravery and leadership. Then he was appointed to command the British forces in Portugal and Spain who were trying to throw Napoleon back into France. In a splendid campaign, marked by several victories, Wellesley drove the French out of Spain and entered France himself. A year later, in 1815, now 1st Duke of Wellington, he crushed Napoleon (see page 15) at Waterloo, one of the greatest battles of history.

After the Napoleonic wars, Wellington was in great demand as a statesman, but he was never able to display the same qualities in home politics as he had in the field of battle, though he was a very good foreign secretary. It was an age of electoral reform, and the country was sharply divided. Wellington never understood the demand for more democratic rights and he opposed it. For a while he was hated, even stoned in the street.

But Britain loves its heroes and by the time young queen Victoria came to the throne in 1837 Wellington was again the most respected man in the country. It is interesting to note that he was no less loved and respected abroad, even in France against whom his greatest victory had been won.

Wren, Sir Christopher (1632–1723), English architect
Wren, who in his long life was to design a great many of the most famous buildings in England, began as a scientist. At twenty-five he was made professor of astronomy in London, and three years later he obtained a similar position at Oxford.

It was during his time as an astronomer, however, that he began to learn about building design, and by the time of the Great Fire of London, in 1666, he had worked his way to being assistant surveyor general to the government. When the smoke from the great conflagration had settled and part of London lay in ruins, the king, Charles II, appointed Wren to reconstruct the wrecked churches and some of the other buildings. One was old St. Paul's, and on the ruins he built the new cathedral, then as now regarded as the greatest church in Britain.

Wren also designed or improved many public and private buildings outside London, including the Sheldonian Theatre in Oxford, Hampton Court Palace, and the Library of Trinity College, Cambridge.

Wright, Wilbur (1867–1912) and Orville (1871–1948), American pioneers of flying

Many attempts had been made by human beings to fly, either with wings attached to their arms or by power-driven craft. But to Wilbur Wright, and his brother Orville, goes the credit for making the first successful flight in a powered aircraft. At Kitty Hawk, in North Carolina, in December 1903, Orville Wright flew nearly 900 feet for about a minute, and then landed safely. It was a great breakthrough, and the brothers followed it up with further experiments. In 1905 Wilbur made a successful circular flight of 24 miles in 38 minutes in Ohio. Soon after this they began to manufacture aeroplanes.

Wycliffe, John (*c.* 1320–1384), English religious reformer

John Wycliffe has been called 'The Morning Star of the Reformation'. This is because he spent most of his life as a preacher attacking the English clergy, especially the bishops and their large retinues, for their high living, their zealous attention to pleasures, and their neglect of their real duties of aiding the sick and needy and spreading the word of God.

He also began to question some of the dogmas of the Church itself, on the grounds that they departed from the true meaning of what Jesus Christ taught. By his own conduct Wycliffe set an example of how the clergy ought to live.

Efforts were made to stop him but he had the protection of John of Gaunt, fourth son of king Edward III, and he remained unharmed. His followers, for there were many who agreed with his ideas, were not so fortunate. After Wycliffe's death they were persecuted, many being burnt at the stake.

Index

The names of all the famous men mentioned in the book are listed, but the main entries are in bold type.

Adam, Robert, **7**
Aethelred I, king of England, 8
Aethelwulf, king of England, 8
Alexander the Great, **7**, 42
Alfred the Great, **8**
Amundsen, Roald, **9**
Andersen, Hans Christian, **9**
Archimedes, **10**
Atahualpa, emperor of Peru, 72
Attila, **10**
Augustus, **11**, 22, 28

Bach, Johann Sebastian, **11**
Bacon, Friar Roger, **12**
Baden-Powell, Lord, **13**
Becket, Thomas à, **13**
Beethoven, Ludwig van, **14**
Bolivar, Simon, **15**
Bonaparte, Napoleon, **15**, 88
Boulton, Matthew, 87
Boyle, the Hon. Robert, **17**
Brian Boru, king of Ireland, 28
Brunel, Sir Marc, **17**
Brunel, Isambard Kingdom, **17**, 55
Brunelleschi, Filippo, **18**
Burghley, Lord William Cecil, **19**
Burns, Robert, **19**

Cabot, John & Sebastian, 23
Caesar, Caius Julius, 11, **20**
Calvin, 24

Canute, king, **22**
Cartier, Jacques, **23**
Catalina, L. Sergius, 28
Caxton, William, **23**
Cecil, see under Burghley
Cervantes, Miguel de, **23**
Chamberlain, Neville, 26
Charles I, king of England, 32
Charles II, king of England, **17**, 88
Charles V, emperor of the Holy Roman Empire, 64
Charlemagne, **24**
Chaucer, Geoffrey, **25**
Chiang Kai-Shek, 81
Chopin, Frederic, **25**
Churchill, Sir Winston, **26**, 41
Cicero, Marcus Tullius, **28**
Collins, Michael, **28**
Columbus, Christopher, **29**, 42, 84, 85
Constantine I, **30**
Constantius, Roman caesar, 30, 39
Cook, Captain James, **31**
Coperinicus, Nicolaus, **31**, 44, 73
Cortez, Hernan, **32**, 72
Crassus, Lucinius, 21
Cromwell, Oliver, **32**
Cyrus, the Great, founder of the Persian empire, 34

Da Gama, Vasco, **34**, 37, 49

Darius I, king of Persia, **34**, 82
Darius III, king of Persia, 7
Darwin, Charles, **35**
David, king of the Hebrews, 78
Da Vinci, Leonardo, **36**, 64
Davy, Sir Humphrey, **37**
Diaz, Bartholomew, **37**, 49
Dickens, Charles, **38**
Diocletian, 29, **38**
Drake, Sir Francis, **39**

Eannes, Gil, 49
Edison, Thomas Alva, **40**
Edmund Ironside, king of England, 22
Edward I, king of England, 46
Edward III, king of England, 25, 89
Edward VI, king of England, 19
Eisenhower, Dwight David, **40**
Emanuel I, king of Portugal, 34
Engels, Friedrich, 63
Erasmus, Desiderius, **41**
Eric the Red, Norwegian Viking chief, 42
Ericsson, Leif, **42**
Euclid, **42**

Ferdinand, king of Spain, 29
Fleming, Sir Alexander, **42**
Franklin, Benjamin, **43**

Galerius, Roman caesar, 39
Galileo, **43**
Garibaldi, Giuseppe, **44**
George I, king of England, 85
Geerts, Geert, see under Erasmus
Genghiz Khan, **45**, 62, 83
Glyndŵr, Owain, **46**

Greco, El, **46**
Gutenburg, Johann, **46**
Guthrum, Viking leader, 9

Hamilcar Barca, Carthaginian general, 47
Hammurabi, **47**
Hannibal, **47**
Henry the Navigator, **49**
Henry II, king of England, 13
Henry IV, king of France, 74
Henry VIII, king of England, 19, 65
Herodotus, **49**
Hiero, king of Syracuse, 10
Hitler, Adolf, 25, **50**, 67, 68
Hudson, Henry, **52**

James II, king of England, 63
Jefferson, Thomas, 43, **52**
Jenner, Dr. Edward, **53**
John I, king of Portugal, 49
John II, king of Portugal, 37
John of Gaunt, 25, 89
Johnson, Dr. Samuel, **53**
Justinian I, 54

Kelvin, Lord William Thomson, 54
Kochel, German scholar, 67
Knox, Dr. John, **55**
Kublai Khan, Mongolian emperor, 62

Lavoisier, Antoine, **55**
Lenin, **56**, 79
Licinius, Roman co-emperor, 30
Lincoln, Abraham, **57**
Lister, Joseph, **58**, 71, 77

Liszt, Franz, 25, 73
Livingstone, Dr. David, **58**
Longfellow, Henry Wadsworth, **59**
Louis XIII, king of France, 74
Louis XIV, king of France, 65
Luther, Martin, 41, 59

Magellan, Ferdinand, 39, **60**
Marconi, Guglielmo, **61**
Mark, Antony, 11
Marlborough, 1st Duke of, 16, 25, **62**, 81
Marx, Karl, **63**
Maximian, Roman co-emperor, 30, 39
Mazarin, French statesman, 74
McKinley, William, American president, 76
Mendelssohn, Felix, 25
Michelangelo, **64**
Molière, **64**
Montezuma, king of the Aztecs, 32
More, Sir Thomas, **65**
Morse, Samuel, **65**
Morton, W. T. G., 58, **66**
Mozart, Wolfgang Amadeus, 14, **66**
Mussolini, Benito, **67**

Napoleon, see under Bonaparte
Narvaez, governor of Cuba, 32
Nelson, Horatio, 15, **68**
Nerva, Roman emperor, 83
Newcomen, Thomas, 87
Newton, Sir Isaac, **69**
Nobel, Alfred, **70**

Nobile, Umberto, Italian explorer, 9

Offa, king of Mercia, 24

Parker, Sir Hyde, 68
Pasteur, Louis, **71**
Peary, Robert, 9
Pericles, **71**
Pepys, Samuel, 17
Philip, king of Macedonia, 7
Pizarro, Francisco, **72**
Polo, Maffeo, 62
Polo, Marco, **62**
Polo, Niccolo, 62
Pompey, 21, 28
Pope Leo I, 11
Plato, 78
Pythagoras, **73**

Rachmaninov, Sergei, **73**
Richelieu, Cardinal le Duc de, **74**
Robespierre, Maximilien, **74**
Roosevelt, Franklin D., 40, 41, **75**
Roosevelt, Theodore, 75, **76**
Rutherford, Lord, **76**

Scott, Captain Robert Falcon, 9
Shakespeare, William, **77**, 78
Shaw, George Bernard, **77**
Socrates, **78**
Solomon, **78**
Stalin, Joseph, **79**
Stanley, Henry M., 59
Stephenson, George, 18, **80**
Stephenson, Robert, 18
Sun Yat-Sen, **80**
Swift, Jonathan, **81**

Tasman, Abel, **81**
Tchaikovski, Peter Ilyitch, **82**
Themistocles, 50, **82**
Theodosius III, Byzantine emperor, 11
Timurlaine, **83**
Titian, Italian painter, 46
Trajan, **83**
Trevithick, Richard, **84**
Trotsky, Russian communist, 79

Van Dieman, governor-general of the Dutch East Indies, 81
Vespucci, Amerigo, **84**
Victor Emanuel III, king of Italy, 67

Von Hindenburg, German president, 51

Waldseemüller, German geographer, 85
Walpole, Sir Robert, **85**
Warren, Dr., 66
Washington, George, **85**
Watt, James, **87**
Weimar, duke of, 12
Wellington, 1st Duke of, 17, **87**
William III, king of England, 63
Wren, Sir Christopher, 17, **88**
Wright, Orville, **89**
Wright, Wilbur, **89**
Wycliffe, John, **89**

Xerxes, king of Persia, 82

In the same series:

Ask me a question

by J. Perry Harvey

All knowledge is exciting and it is quite remarkable how much you can learn without even thinking about it. You can have a lot of fun, too, from the many and varied quizzes which make up *Ask me a question*. They lead on to all kinds of interesting points of discovery and, at the same time, provide hours of amusement.

The Zebra Book of Facts for Girls

The Zebra Book of Facts for Boys

compiled by Cyril and Joyce Parsons

These books contain all kinds of facts about World History and Geography, Science and Mathematics, National and Local Government. For enthusiasts there are sporting records, nature notes, codes and ciphers and First Aid information. There is a special section for cyclists and a number of suggestions for things to do on a wet day or on a long journey. They are, in fact, packed with fascinating information which boys and girls will find most useful.